Does God Have a Strategy?

Does God Have a Strategy?
A Dialogue

Phillip Cary

Jean-François Phelizon

With translation by
Anne François

 CASCADE *Books* • Eugene, Oregon

DOES GOD HAVE A STRATEGY?
A Dialogue

Copyright © 2015 Phillip Cary and Jean-François Phelizon. All rights reserved. Except for brief quotations in critical publications or reviews, no part of this book may be reproduced in any manner without prior written permission from the publisher. Write: Permissions. Wipf and Stock Publishers, 199 W. 8th Ave., Suite 3, Eugene, OR 97401.

Cascade Books
An Imprint of Wipf and Stock Publishers
199 W. 8th Ave., Suite 3
Eugene, OR 97401

www.wipfandstock.com

ISBN 13: 978-1-4982-2395-9

Cataloguing-in-Publication Data

Cary, Phillip, and Jean-François Phelizon.

    Does God have a strategy? a dialogue / Phillip Cary and Jean-François Phelizon, with translation by Anne François.

    x + 170 p. ; 23 cm. Includes bibliographical references.

    ISBN 13: 978-1-4982-2395-9

    1. Strategic planning. 2. Strategy—Theology. 3. Strategy—Philosophy. I. Title.

HD30.28 .C3774 2015

Manufactured in the U.S.A.   10/15/2015

Biblical quotations are from *The Holy Bible, English Standard Version*, copyright 2001, by Crossway Bibles, a publishing ministry of Good News Publishers. Used by permission. All rights reserved.

For all who believe.

And for the others.

Contents

Preface | ix

1. A Strategy of Blessing? | 1
2. Three Jealous Brothers | 22
3. Religions and Revolutions | 48
4. Truth, Tolerance, and Utopia | 64
5. Paradigms of God | 87
6. The God of Redemption | 105
7. Jesus and the Church in History | 133

Bibliography | 169

Preface

My friend Jean-François Phelizon writes books about strategy; I write books about God. I suppose it is not surprising that he would ask me whether God has a strategy, and that this would result in a book. Jean-François wrote to me in French, I responded in English, and then we asked my colleague Anne François, Professor of French at Eastern University in Pennsylvania, to provide a translation, which I revised and finalized.

What I do find rather surprising is the shape of our disagreement. Jean-François and I made a point of disagreeing like friends, but disagree we did, and in the book that follows you can feel us pushing hard against each other. I have to say, I enjoyed this. I often felt like I was arguing with a son of Voltaire, who is the source of many old arguments against orthodox Christianity that are now recycled by the so-called "new atheists," but who is more interesting than they are because he was a man of deep religious hope in a God of universal goodness, a deist with a warm heart. Still, I am the kind of Christian who harbors suspicions about the modern, Enlightenment view of universal reason, which Voltaire represented so splendidly; so I ended up playing postmodernist (of a sort) to Jean-François' modernist. It is, to my mind, a surprising new inflection of an old disagreement.

What also strikes me as surprising about our disagreement is how it reaches not only "across the pond" but over the channel. The new atheists—to pick on them again—all write in English, paying little attention to what is thought on the other side of the English channel but getting a large audience on both sides of the Atlantic, that little body of water that does less to separate the British and the Americans than the channel does to separate the French from them both. So here in this book you have the unusual phenomenon of an American Protestant arguing with a French heir of the

Preface

Enlightenment for whom the Roman Catholic Church is still "*the* Church." And, as often happens these days, the Protestant is less critical of Roman Catholicism than is the heir of the Enlightenment.

Jean-François and I have agreed to let him have the last word in this book—as well as giving me the first—but as you will see, the last word certainly does not resolve our differences. We are pushing back at each other to the end. I do hope that the *way* we push back at each other illustrates, in a small way, something about God's grand strategy, which has to do with how differences may remain differences without becoming destructive. But how that may be is itself a matter we disagree about.

Disagreement itself leads to strategy, which originates in the art of war but has now become integral to the art of negotiation as well. You always have to have a strategy for dealing with people with whom you have serious differences. As a consequence, what we think about the possibility of a divine strategy, which must be a strategy for the universe as a whole, will affect our strategy for pushing back against those we disagree with—giving shape to the manner as well as the content of the disagreement. We want to practice disagreeing like friends.

I have tried to learn from my friend something about the very notion of strategy, on which I am no expert. And he has had to hear from me a great deal about the Christian view of God, some of which is very old but much of which must have sounded rather new. Over the course of the discussion we have many things to say about metaphysics, epistemology, politics, and history. But the great question—with its postmodern inflection to my ears—is whether the framework of one particular religion could possibly be the context in which to understand a divine strategy for the whole world. I think the strategy of God is necessarily particular in that way, because it must be a strategy with a particular place in history, starting from a particular people with their particular hope and faith in their particular Messiah, and flowing outward from there to reach the whole world. Jean-François resists becoming so parochial, if I may put it that way. But he will be speaking for himself soon enough.

What I would like to commend to you, here where I have the first word, is the following conversation about why we may have hope for humanity, and what our participation in that hope requires of us even as we push against those whose hopes take a different form from ours. We must not give up hope, but we should also not stop pushing.

–Phillip Cary

1

A Strategy of Blessing?

Phillip Cary—Does God have a strategy? That is an interesting question, for a number of reasons. To begin with, the very idea that God could have a strategy might seem odd. In the monotheist conception, God is omnipotent, the creator of all things. Shouldn't God simply be in control of everything, always getting his way? "For who can resist his will?" as the apostle says (Rom 9:19). Who can say no to God?

And yet it is evident—also from a monotheist conception—that we do say no to God all the time. What God creates can talk back to him, resist him, flee him, disbelieve in him, even curse him. The possibility of this "no" opens up the possibility of divine strategy. We can say no to God, and he has to deal with that. Or I should say, he chooses to deal with that. He chooses to be the kind of creator whose creatures can say no to him, and therefore one who has to adopt a strategy for dealing with beings who resist him, with recalcitrant wills that oppose his purposes in the world. You might say, he chooses to create an interesting world—one that would be interesting also to him.

At least so it is in the narrative of the Bible, from which I propose to derive my thoughts about divine strategy. The later theological traditions of Judaism and Christianity have a great deal to add to this, of course, and at a further remove so also does the theological tradition of Islam. Nearly all of us in Europe and America stand, as it were, downstream from the Bible, within the influence of its derivative religious traditions—even the many of us who are no longer believers in them. Whenever we think about God we

Does God Have a Strategy?

drink, as it were, from what these traditions carry to us, across the centuries, from this primal source. But by the same token, it is always possible to go back to the source—the religious traditions themselves frequently urge us to do so. When we do that, we bring our traditions with us—we should not be naïve and unaware of this. Even ex-Christians still read the Bible like Christians, and ex-Jews like Jews. But we inevitably do read, fascinated by this source which is the beginning of so much of our thinking down to this day. So I am a Christian reading like a Christian, but trying to go back to this source which pre-dates Christianity—which is a very Christian thing to do.

The source is a story about God and these human creatures of his who keep saying no to him in various ways. And yes, he has to develop a strategy to deal with this.

Jean-François Phelizon—It seems to me we should begin by defining what strategy is.

1. In the broadest sense, strategy (or rather, *conceptual* strategy, which I will contrast in a moment with *operational* strategy) is the art of moving a social group: a nation, an army, a business, for example. Its aim is to obtain real or supposed advantages that the group could not obtain otherwise, except by chance. It implies a *direction*, from which there necessarily follows a common rule of action. Why a direction? There is in Chinese an interesting character, *dào* (sometimes transliterated *tao*), which means road, way, teaching, and by extension, to lead, to educate. It is composed of two radicals, one meaning *to go* and the other *forward*. I think *dào* is close to the concept of strategy, precisely because the strategy of a group is nothing other than a road traveled in common, which presupposes a common direction and a common rule. Hence, *a strategy is a guideline*. It is a guideline to which everyone is held—and to which everyone is expected to hold themselves.

When different social groups, in the name of what they call their interests, lay claim to the same resources, they come into conflict and their strategies are usually in competition with one another. Sports teams, businesses, armies, and to a certain extent religious institutions constitute communities that I describe as *agonistic*, and their conceptual strategy is thus the rule of action for an agonistic group.

For entities that are agonistic and competing with each other (that is to say, *antagonistic*), conflict is at once legitimate, inevitable, and sustained.

1 – A Strategy of Blessing?

It is legitimate, because each entity is certain that it is in the right and that the behavior and claims of the *other* are utterly unacceptable. It is inevitable, because the opponent does not want to "listen to reason" and one can't back down without losing something essential: interests, identity, honor. And it is sustained, because while one ascribes to the other the responsibility of surrendering when beaten, one anticipates that hostilities will arise whenever one shows weakness.

As a rule of action, conceptual strategy is related to constraint, an obligation to behave in a certain way. It is inspired by what is relevant, and is connected to politics. It is contrasted with operational strategy, which certainly pursues objectives compatible with the rule of action but takes more account of risks and opportunities. Operational strategy then opens out onto tactics, whose degree of freedom and choice of means stem entirely from contingent circumstances.

In fact, although every strategic concept imposes a direction on a social group as well as on the strategist who leads it, the conduct of the strategy should be constrained as little as possible. The Chinese author Sun Tzu is right in saying that the conduct of military operations is like the flow of water. Water is by nature shapeless; it always flows around the heights in order to pour into the depths. Likewise in battle, the thing to do is to avoid the enemy's strong points and attack his weak spots instead. More broadly, it is a matter of making tactics depend on how the situation develops, adapting to what could be called *the infinite variety of circumstances*.

2. Conceptual strategy is analyzed in terms of *necessities*, operational strategy in terms of *objectives*, and tactics in terms of *opportunities*.

At the operational level, the strategist establishes objectives. He must find a solution to the problem that he sets for himself or that has been set for him, which means he must work out a combination of basic effects—offensive or defensive—corresponding to the maneuver he envisions to arrive at the desired result. He must put in place means that, once activated, become forces that can be opposed to those of his adversary. But it is not enough to dispose of means. The good strategist is the one who manages to find the time and space he needs. He is thus the one who, to varying degrees, knows how to make time and terrain his allies.

For the tactician, by contrast, nothing is ever set. It is only by accepting situations as they are—and through them the principle of reality—that he can triumph over them. To humble oneself before experience remains the first and supreme commandment of the mind. So when it's time to act,

Does God Have a Strategy?

the first task of the strategist is to determine his degrees of freedom. If he's lacking in that area, then it's absolutely imperative for him to "break the game wide open." In this way conceptual vision is relentlessly refined by the facts. In other words, *the dogmatism of the strategic concept must be answered by the pragmatism with which it is put into effect.*

Strategy may be reducible to a simple idea, but because in the end it comes down to contingent circumstances the conduct of strategy turns out to be infinitely complex. As Napoleon famously said, the art of war is simple but it's all in the execution. Which means, in the view of Marshall Foch, that facts must take precedence over ideas, deeds over words, and execution over theory. Also, that means the strategist's responsibility to be vigilant extends beyond refining his vision. It also includes seizing opportunities within the framework of a "necessity": conducting the strategy of the group over which he has assumed leadership.

3. Rereading the Bible now, it is easy to find lots of references to objectives that are to be achieved, but harder to spot traces of a conceptual strategy. Is there an overall direction to the history of the people of Israel or to the early history of Christianity? Do these histories have a meaning? Do they follow a guideline? Do they give expression to a dynamic leading to a definite result in a given direction? This deserves analysis and discussion.

It really is necessary to make a distinction between what Christians call the Old and New Testaments. The Old Testament tells the story of the Jewish people by way of various remarkable episodes. Especially in the Torah, the divine teaching that according to tradition was handed down by Moses in the Pentateuch, and at each stage of their existence, one has the impression of the Jewish people being "led" by God; whereas the New Testament looks more like a message of justice and peace addressed by Christ to all human beings. Perhaps one must conclude that the Old Testament is subordinated to a strategy (more operational than conceptual) and that the New Testament is situated at an entirely conceptual level.

Phillip Cary—Using your definition and terminology, and combining it with the way Christian theology reads the Bible, I would describe divine strategy as follows. At the highest level, God's *conceptual strategy* is to bless the human race with life, despite our opposition. We human creatures are all *antagonists* of God's strategy insofar as we are heirs of Cain and Abel (Gen 4:1–16), for we have become antagonists of one another, preferring that other humans die so that we might live. Like Cain, we want God's favor

1 – A Strategy of Blessing?

and blessing for ourselves, not for others, and so we kill them. Our antagonism to God's strategy is our murderousness. The *direction* of God's strategy, his way or *dào*, is opposite to our direction toward death for others. It is blessing and life for others, even at great cost to oneself. This strategy is carried out most fully on the cross of Christ. The *rule of action* of divine strategy is, in a word, love. By this I mean the kind of work that grows from the desire that others might live and be blessed rather than die and get out of our way. Or one could say: love is the enacted hope that I might find in the other a friend rather than an enemy or a slave.

At the next level, in God's *operational strategy*, his primary *objective* is to reverse the kind of relationship we see between Cain and Abel by using one part of the human race to bring life and blessing to others. This strategy is founded on what theology calls "the doctrine of election," which is to say, the doctrine of what God chooses or elects. In the biblical doctrine of election, God chooses some to bless others, as for example Abraham is chosen to be a blessing for "all the families of the earth" (Gen 12:3). In the Old Testament this means that Israel in particular, the chosen people descended from Abraham, Isaac and Jacob, is to be a blessing for the Gentiles. To each of these three ancestors God makes a version of the same promise: "in your offspring shall all the nations of the earth be blessed" (Gen 22:18, 26:4, and 28:14). The word for "nations" here is *goyim*, often translated "Gentiles"—a word that covers all non-Jews. The idea is that it is a good thing for the Gentiles that the Jews are the chosen people.

Of course the Gentiles often do not see it that way, so in this respect also God's strategy encounters antagonists. The opposition can be quite literal, as the nations often aim to destroy Israel. Then it becomes an *objective* of God's strategy to defend his people against their enemies. We see much of this in the Old Testament. It needs to be emphasized that this is not the primary objective of divine strategy, but a secondary objective that serves the primary objective: God cannot bless all nations through Israel if Israel does not exist, so God defends Israel from the murderousness of her neighbors. The Bible connects these two objectives by joining curse to blessing in God's words to Abraham, which I take to define God's operational strategy: "I will bless those who bless you, and him who dishonors you I will curse, and in you all the families of the earth shall be blessed" (Gen 12:3). There is both curse and blessing, but the curse is for the sake of the blessing, as God defends his people *in order to* bless others.

Does God Have a Strategy?

And the biblical story gets yet more complicated than that. For there are many episodes in the Old Testament in which God takes sides *against* the people of Israel when they rebel against him. He brings armies against them, hands them over to their enemies, and sends them into exile. Here we see a third objective of divine strategy: God disciplines his people so that they are obedient to his strategy. Always when defeat or disaster overtakes Israel, the Old Testament sees this not as meaningless misfortune, but as punishment by a king who loves his people or (to use another biblical image) a father who loves his children. Here the deep and heart-wrenching complication is that the recalcitrant others who oppose God's strategy are his own beloved, "the apple of his eye" (Deut 32:10). So the divine strategy is never as simple as: God fights for his people until their enemies are defeated. That would be contrary to the whole direction of divine strategy, which is to bless others rather than defeat them.

Again, most of humanity does not see it this way. The Jews are often resented for thinking of themselves as the chosen people, as if this were their idea, a form of arrogance that is insulting to the rest of us. So the story of jealous nations trying to destroy Israel continues, alas, long after the Old Testament. In this regard Christians bear a particular responsibility, becoming in an especially deep way the recalcitrant others who are antagonists of God's strategy. Where the Jews have been concerned, it has been very common for Christians to think like Cain, who was so jealous of the favor God showed his brother that he killed him. Thus Christians have supposed that in order to receive salvation, grace, and blessing, Christians must be the true chosen people, not the Jews, and that the Jews deserve death for saying otherwise. As a Christian theologian, therefore, I am especially insistent on its being good news for all nations that the Jews are God's chosen people. For only when Christians have thoroughly understood this good news are Jews safe from Christian anti-Semitism.

The further we delve into these complications the more we move from strategy to *tactics*. Because tactics are so various, conforming to the contours of a particular battlefield (or like water finding a channel downhill in a particular landscape, to borrow Sun Tzu's metaphor) it is very difficult to generalize about the direction they will take. But we can name a few characteristic *opportunities* that arise from the general rule of action that I have summed up in the one word, *love*. When those recalcitrant others annoy you, be patient; when they are needy, be generous. When they offend you, forgive; when you offend them, ask forgiveness. Even when you must

1 – A Strategy of Blessing?

defend yourself against them, seek their good, not their destruction. These are some of the opportunities I suppose the Apostle Paul had in mind when he wrote, "Love is patient and kind; love does not envy or boast; it is not arrogant or rude. It does not insist on its own way; it is not irritable or resentful" (1 Cor 13:4–5). All of this is much easier said than done, of course, but that is how it always is with tactics. Here Napoleon's saying certainly applies: it's all in the execution.

So now we have had a look at the *opportunities* of tactics as well as the *objectives* of operational strategy. Let me conclude by mentioning the *necessity* that I see in God's conceptual strategy. By this I mean not the necessity of need but the necessity of what cannot be otherwise. In God what cannot be otherwise is that he is good. Hence it is not an accident that curse serves blessing in the divine strategy, rather than the other way round. For it cannot be that God's ultimate aim or direction is to bring evil upon the human race that he created and loves. In other words, we can say: any conception of a God who is not good—including good *to us*—is a conception of a God who does not exist.

Jean-François Phelizon—Strategy of course has to be translated into a set of actions that aim at countering some kind of resistance. In this sense every strategy is carried out *against others*. But who are these "others"? The adversary may be internal or external. In other words, one may want to conquer a new territory or one may want to "put one's house in order." Recall the Gospel, "No city or house divided against itself will stand" (Matt 12:25), as well as Abraham Lincoln's famous "House Divided" speech, which takes this biblical passage as its motto.

The nature of the resistance one encounters varies, depending on whether the adversary is internal or external. The resistance you describe is that of human beings against the will of God. God, you say, has chosen that we can resist him. Must one conclude that he has created a world of recalcitrant people who would be his adversaries? That his opposition to the human race is a sort of game—might I say, a game of strategy like chess? To talk about strategy is to talk about uncertainty of success. In the match that pits him against humans, it's clear that God makes up a team all by himself. But what are the prospects for the opposing team, made up of the human race? Is it a fair game? Does it have only one rule? Does God playing against us leave us any chance of winning? Or is he simply trying to manipulate us?

Does God Have a Strategy?

But there's more. This lovely picture of human beings who have the choice to resist the divine will puts us on an equal footing with God. Can we really picture that? Doesn't it show great arrogance to believe such a thing? Resisting God seems to me a very unlikely picture—indeed unreal, because in reality it happens often enough that one can't even challenge a religion. State religions continue to exist, not to mention the resulting social restrictions. (Catholicism was for a long time a state religion, although the second Vatican council in 1965 solemnly declared that the human person has a right to religious freedom.) So is it really possible to resist God when one can't even question a dogma, a supposedly divine law—or for the Muslims a *sharia*? Must one conclude that religions are nothing but human constructions *opposed* to the will of God?

Treating the conceptual strategy of God means asking what kind of action it is supposed to promote and within what guiding framework. But if you want to deal with the operational strategy of God, then you have to ask if he really does have objectives and, if so, what are they? For example, whether he has one specific strategy for the Jews (which might be deducible from the Torah) and another for Christians (coming from the Gospels). Or again, whether he carries out one strategy with certain human beings (those whom he has chosen) or with the whole human race. You claim that God can "deal with" the action of completely recalcitrant human beings who do not even believe in him. What a lovely paradox! With regard to the direction chosen by God as it is found in the New Testament, I think it is worth rereading the following passage in Luke, because it seems to me to be diametrically opposed to what is represented by a strategic concept:

> And he lifted up his eyes on his disciples and said: "Blessed are you who are poor, for yours is the kingdom of God. Blessed are you who are hunger now, for you shall be satisfied. Blessed are you who weep now, for you shall laugh. But I say to you who hear: Love your enemies, do good to those who hate you, bless those who curse you, pray for those who abuse you. To one who strikes you on the cheek, offer the other also, and from one who takes away your cloak do not withhold your tunic" (Luke 6:20–29).

Is there anything more contrary to traditional strategic action, in fact, than to *do good to those who hate you*? Is there anything more extravagant than to *love your enemies*?

Yet one finds there is a gap between the guideline and the rule of action or, more precisely, between the teachings of Christ and the way Christianity

1 – A Strategy of Blessing?

has interpreted them over the course of its history. Let us reread now some passages from Matthew: "If you forgive others their trespasses, your heavenly Father will also forgive you, but if you do not forgive others their trespasses, neither will your Father forgive your trespasses" (6:14). "Look at the birds of the air: they neither sow nor reap nor gather into barns, and yet your heavenly Father feeds them. Are you not of more value than they?" (6:26). "Therefore do not be anxious about tomorrow, for tomorrow will be anxious for itself. Sufficient for the day is its own trouble" (6:34). "Go and learn what this means: 'I desire mercy, and not sacrifice.' For I came not to call the righteous, but sinners" (9:13). "Whoever loves father or mother more than me is not worthy of me, and whoever loves son or daughter more than me is not worthy of me" (10:37). The general rule of action stemming from the New Testament is really quite far from ordinary human actions. It gives the impression of prescribing something that never happens in reality. (On the other hand, it resembles the rule of certain Asian religions such as Buddhism and Confucianism—a point to which I will return).

Could it be that God's "strategy," as inferred from the Gospels, is utopian? In any case it looks paradoxical (not to say subversive) in the famous parable of the Workers at the Eleventh Hour, which has given rise to a great deal of contradictory commentary:

> The kingdom of heaven is like a master of a house who went out early in the morning to hire laborers for his vineyard. After agreeing with the laborers for a denarius a day, he sent them into his vineyard. And going out about the third hour he saw others standing idle in the marketplace, and to them he said, "You go into the vineyard too, and whatever is right I will give you." So they went. Going out again about the sixth hour and the ninth hour, he did the same. And about the eleventh hour he went out and found others standing. And he said to them, "Why do you stand here idle all day?" They said to him, "Because no one has hired us." He said to them, "You go into the vineyard too." And when evening came, the owner of the vineyard said to his foreman, "Call the laborers and pay them their wages, beginning with the last, up to the first." And when those hired about the eleventh hour came, each of them received a denarius. Now when those hired first came, they thought they would receive more, but each of them also received a denarius. And on receiving it they grumbled at the master of the house, saying, "These last worked only one hour, and you have made them equal to us who have borne the burden of the day and the scorching heat." But he replied to one of them,

"Friend, I am doing you no wrong. Did you not agree with me for a denarius? Take what belongs to you and go. I choose to give to this last worker as I give to you. Am I not allowed to do what I choose with what belongs to me? Or do you begrudge my generosity?' [literally: "Is your eye evil because I am good?"] So the last will be first, and the first last (Matt 20:1–16).

What conclusions should one draw from this at a practical level? Should Christians abandon every notion of effort, of work, of justice? Should their only ambition be to be *last*?

And there are other important questions for us still to answer. For example, is "blessing others" a general objective or is it really rather a guideline? In the first case, human beings remain free but we cannot really say that this general objective represents a strategy. In the second, it is perhaps a divine strategy, but what about the freedom to be and to think? As for those who might be "chosen," to what category do they belong? Are they pursuing a strategy for themselves, supported by God, or are they instruments of God pursuing his own strategy? Finally, is there continuity between the Old and New Testaments in the matter of strategy? We should not neglect to delve into this.

Moreover, I notice that this concept of "the blessing of the Gentiles" is not found in the Gospels and especially not in the Qur'an, where instead God appears to be highly directive. As he is thought to "command" the human race he is in fact entitled to punish it, especially in cases of *infidelity*. "Allah is Hearer, Knower" (Qur'an 2:181).[1] Allah "revealed the Qur'an, a guidance for mankind" (2:185). "And he whom Allah guideth, for him there can be no misleader" (39:37). "And who goeth further astray than he who followeth his lust without guidance from Allah?" (28:50). "Your Lord proclaimed: If ye give thanks, I will give you more; but if ye are thankless, lo! my punishment is dire" (14:7). Hence the question that arises is: how can blessing people against their will constitute a strategy?

Reflecting on God's strategy certainly raises a great many questions. Might it be true that human beings "encompass nothing of His knowledge save what He will"? (Qur'an 2:255).

Phillip Cary—Yes, God's strategy is odd. It has to be. If, in a murderous world, God's operational strategy is to choose some people to bless others, then he cannot behave simply like an ancient king leading his people to war

---

1. Translations of the Qur'an are from Pickthall, *Glorious Koran*.

1 – A Strategy of Blessing?

or a general leading one army to defeat another. He is more like a father trying to keep his warring children from killing each other. He cannot simply join the fight on one side or another, but neither can he simply avoid the fighting, as if it were sufficient to stand aside and wish everyone would be nice to each other. His strategy must be complex, and the rule of action called "love" must often go in difficult and unexpected directions, such as loving enemies, forgiving offenders, and being generous to the undeserving.

This will not always look like justice—at least not if justice is understood in terms of equality. A love that goes in such strange directions cannot treat everyone equally. Sometimes, being extravagantly generous, it will look like favoritism—just as sometimes, in forgiving murderous enemies, it will look like helplessness ("Father, forgive them, for they know not what they do," says Jesus from the cross, in Luke 23:34). If this is paradoxical, it is the kind of paradox that should delight a tactician, who looks for reversals and ironies on the battlefield, where weakness can have unexpected strengths and exaggeration can restore a kind of balance. I put these works of love in the category of tactics, because they are ways of seizing opportunities for the strategy of blessing the recalcitrant others who oppose our strategies.

Of course it is a question how our strategies could ever be God's. But if God has chosen a people for himself, then one of his tasks as strategist is to find a way to use them for his strategy of blessing others. The practical answer to this question comes in part as people take the opportunity to learn the difficult kind of tactics that carry out a strategy of blessing others. Jesus' parable of the workers in the vineyard, which you quote from the Gospel of Matthew, presents such an opportunity.

The parable highlights a certain kind of jealousy or envy that seems to have caught Jesus' attention. He makes a point of the master of the house insisting that no injustice has been done, no one has been defrauded or paid less than a fair wage—so that he can say, "Friend, I am doing you no wrong" (Matt 20:13). The challenge of the parable comes when the master adds: "Is your eye evil because I am good?" (Matt 20:15). The translation here is quite exact. The evil eye in the original Greek probably reflects a Hebrew idiom in which something that displeases people is said to be "evil in their eyes" (e.g., Gen 21:11, 1 Sam 8:6). It makes for a vivid picture of envy: God is good and blesses you, but this is evil in my eyes, because I am displeased that you should be better off than I am. What Jesus highlights here is a view of others that goes back to Cain, who saw God accept his

Does God Have a Strategy?

brother's worship and it was evil in his eyes—so evil that he would rather kill his brother than let him live to enjoy such blessing.

The same kind of jealousy shows up at the end of Jesus' parable of the Prodigal Son, when the prodigal's elder brother is angry at their father for killing the fatted calf and celebrating the return of "this son of yours," as he contemptuously calls him (Luke 15:30). His brother has come back to his father's blessing, and this is evil in his sight. The parable ends with the father trying to persuade his son to see things differently, saying, "It is fitting to celebrate and be glad, for this brother of yours was dead and is alive; he was lost and is found" (Luke 15:32). The question it leaves us with is: can we be glad that God blesses the other or will our eye be evil like Cain's, so that we regret that our brother is alive, not dead?

I think that Jesus is presenting us with a kind of commentary on the stories of jealous brothers in Genesis, which culminates in Joseph's brothers asking him to forgive them—the first time this word is used in the Bible (Gen 50:17). They had tried to kill him out of jealousy, but Joseph famously reassures them, "you meant evil against me, but God meant it for good" (Gen 50:20). Their eye was evil, we could say, but God was good. And why? "To bring it about that many people should be kept alive, as they are today." It is a reversal of the story of Cain: because of Joseph, his murderous brothers and all their children are alive, not dead.

Jesus wants us to realize, I think, that such a reversal happened once before in Genesis, in an episode that lies at the foundation of Israel's existence. Earlier in his parable, when the prodigal son is returning home, his father—who represents God in the parable—sees him from a distance and runs to him, falls on his neck and kisses him (Luke 15:20). The striking phrase "fell on his neck" is often left out of translations, replaced with some vaguer term such as "embrace," but it is a key to the parable, for it belongs to a sequence of verbs that occurs nowhere else in the Bible except one place in Genesis: where one jealous brother sees another returning home, and runs to him, embraces him and falls on his neck, kisses him and weeps (Gen 33:4). It is an older brother glad to see his younger brother alive, not dead—just as the father in Jesus' parable hopes. It is a striking reversal, for the younger brother had fled years earlier precisely because his older brother wanted to kill him (Gen 27:41). It is all the more striking in that the younger brother is Jacob, the chosen one who is ancestor of all the tribes of Israel (who are named after him, as he received the new name "Israel" just before this episode, in Genesis 32:28), whereas the older brother is Esau,

1 – A Strategy of Blessing?

the one from whom Jacob had stolen the blessing of his father (in an important episode narrated in Genesis 27). You have to expect the children of Israel to identify with Jacob, the chosen one who has the blessing, and nearly all readers of the Bible have subsequently done so. Yet Jesus is suggesting that if you want to behave like your Father in heaven—to carry out his strategy, we may say—then you need to be like Esau, the murderous one who changes course and ends up doing what the father in Jesus' parable does, running to the younger brother and falling on his neck and kissing him, because he is so glad that this blessed other is alive, not dead.

In Jesus' reading of the Scriptures of Israel, it is Esau who begins to reverse the legacy of murderous jealousy that originates with Cain. The parable of the Prodigal Son suggests that if we are to participate in the strategy by which God blesses others, we must become like Esau, glad that the other whom God has blessed is alive not dead, rather than aspiring to be like Jacob, the chosen one who succeeds in getting possession of the blessing. This is a hard pill to swallow. Instead of directing us toward God's blessing, this strategy directs us toward the blessing of others—including those who have wronged us. It puts us at risk, not like a wise general who knows when to risk his troops in order to defeat the enemy, but like a despised outcast who rescues an enemy from death—like the Samaritan in Jesus' most famous parable, a man unclean under Jewish law, who is moved by compassion to save the life of one of the enemies of his people (Luke 10:30–37). "You go, and do likewise," he concludes (Luke 10:37), as if expecting the people of God to emulate a Samaritan—or as if the children of Jacob should want to be like Esau!

Love of enemies, forgiving the wrongdoer, and extravagant generosity are only a few of the tactics that follow from the divine strategy of choosing some for the blessing of others—a strategy that must operate not by defeating enemies but by overcoming our murderous jealousies. I have already pointed out how Christian anti-Semitism can be murderously jealous of the blessing God has given to his chosen people, the Jews. Christians have tried to play Jacob and steal the blessing from these sons of Jacob (there are so many ironies when you see the world in terms of biblical stories!) and it has made us murderous like Cain or like the elder brother in Jesus' parable, who regrets that his blessed brother is not dead. It is to these biblical stories of jealous brothers that I return, again and again, when I want to understand the shape of divine strategy in history.

Does God Have a Strategy?

Jean-François Phelizon—Thanks to your certitudes, it seems to me you have taken the lead. I am more skeptical, "recalcitrant" perhaps, and I'm starting further back, with many questions still on my mind. So I return to the concept of strategy in relation to the theme that concerns us, which is whether or not there is such a thing as a divine strategy.

1. Strategy can be defined in two rather different ways, one very general (conceptual strategy) and the other essentially military (operational strategy). If the principle of "nestedness" is accepted, which I'll expand upon in just a moment, then the first encompasses the second.

In the broadest sense, strategy is a way, a goal; so it implies a direction. Not a vague direction such as the way to happiness, but a true change of course for which *an agonistic group, if necessary, is ready to put up a fight.* Of course, to follow a direction there must be adequate means. The means come within the purview of operational strategy and tactics; they have to be proportionate to the objectives set. To have a strategy without disposing of means is just dreaming. To have a guideline without taking account of means at one's disposal is deluding oneself. But to dispose of means without having a direction is to lack a strategy.

In both senses of the word—and corresponding to its etymology—strategy is *collective*. Hence to speak of "individual strategy" is not quite proper usage but metaphorical. Because strategy is a direction that is collective, it is imposed as a rule of action, which may come within the purview of morality or ethics. Thus to preach Christian morality or Buddhist morality is a necessary but not sufficient condition for the existence of a divine strategy.

An agonistic group does not take a given direction by chance; in order to act it needs a guide, a "leader"—a prophet. The earthly leader is indeed present in the hierarchy of the military or of the Catholic church, but not really within the Jewish or Protestant religion. But where is God in all this? Is he opposed to human beings or is he rather their supreme leader? If he leads the human race then the "resistance" he encounters is internal. But then how can he be the leader of two antagonistic groups at the same time (for example, Christians and Muslims)? In any case, he seems quite alone in relation to the human race and the countless "recalcitrant" creatures that he has nonetheless created.

Since strategy is collective and derives from an agonistic group, it is inevitably carried out against other groups (or possibly within one and the same group that is divided against itself). This *other* is not merely

1 – A Strategy of Blessing?

"recalcitrant," it is unbearable, intolerable, hateful, and one of the objectives of operational strategy is to reduce it, to bring it under control, indeed to suppress it. Here we come upon the problem of the habitual (and normal) intolerance of religions. It is hard to admit that a tolerant religion (such as certain Asian religions) follows a strategy, precisely because it is not opposed to the others. Conversely, one can admit that the "Abrahamic" religions have strategies because over the ages they have all fought among themselves, with all three displaying the most extreme intolerance. So of which religion is God the "leader"? Precisely when a religion does not admit that an unbeliever may *resist*, does it not distance itself *infinitely* from God?

2. Though the Jewish religion and the Christian religions are founded on the Torah and the Gospels, these foundational "sacred" texts have been followed by many other texts forming the body of doctrine that has little by little diluted these religions. In order to appreciate the strategy that may originate from the foundational texts, one has to read the Bible together with later Jewish texts and consider the history of Christianity from the composition of the New Testament up to the present day. In other words, one must take account of the great many supplementary writings that these religions have produced, recognized, and incorporated over the centuries.

Now the question of whether God has a strategy is different from the question of whether a religion has a strategy. In theory at least, God could have a strategy (expressed for example in the New Testament) that might be different from that carried out by the temporal power that represents him on earth. To put it another way, nothing says that the strategy followed by a pope is a divine strategy, or that it is consistent with the strategy that originates from the Gospels.

In addition, you have spoken of a kind of *continuity* between the two sacred texts of the Bible, as Christians consider it. If it exists, it must be a matter of the continuity between a "movie" (the Old Testament) and a "snapshot" (the New Testament), which is further extended by a history that is largely secular. In any case, what has happened after the snapshot shows that the actions of Christianity have not always been consistent with the precepts of the New Testament—far from it!

3. If strategy is a direction, if it imposes a rule of action, it cannot allow this rule to change except at the risk of thereby making the strategy it is supposed to support incoherent. My sense is that there is a collective rule of action originating from the Old Testament and that this rule is rather consistent over time. On the other hand, I do not really see continuity in the rule of action originating from the New Testament.

I return to the principle of "nestedness." It could be that God has a strategy and that human beings have other strategies that serve his (or not), a little like a general carrying out a strategy and subordinates who have strategies of their own that are narrower but thought to be consistent with the guidelines he has put forth. This principle can explain how in the Old Testament, David and others have "micro-strategies" that ultimately go in the direction of God's general strategy for the Jewish people. For when this is not the case, history shows that the Lord imposes sanctions (such as exile in Babylon or the destruction of the temple in Jerusalem).

This "nestedness" of one strategy within another does not seem to exist as far as concerns the history of the Christian religions. At the point where the Catholic Church became *abusive*, there was no divine sanction but something more prosaic: human protests, indignation, revolt, and finally dissent (with the emergence of Luther and Calvin in particular).

Phillip Cary—The issues you raise will require me to set forth a number of fundamental concepts that will be important for our subsequent discussion.

1. *Religions.* We can begin with the distinctiveness of the monotheist religions, and of Christianity in particular. Very significantly, the three great monotheist religions, Judaism, Christianity, and Islam, are historical kin. Not only did they arise from one another (Christianity being impossible without Judaism, Islam impossible without both Judaism and Christianity), they all think of themselves as going back to the same fundamental relationship between God and Abraham. Hence they are rightly called Abrahamic religions. The stories they tell about their own identity are consequently intertwined. Christianity cannot tell its own story without telling a story also about the Jews, and Islam cannot tell its story without speaking of Abraham, Ishmael, Moses, and Jesus, as well as the Torah and the Gospels (terms whose Arabic equivalents appear very frequently in the Qur'an).

The very fact that they all have a story to tell about themselves and about their God suggests the likelihood of a strategy, a direction, a *dénouement* toward which their stories are headed. I will be very interested in this connection between story and strategy. This is tied to the linear view of time that prevails in the monotheist religions, where history is conceived as

1 – A Strategy of Blessing?

headed toward some kind of end or culmination or fulfillment, like a good story. This is an especially strong component of Christianity.

By contrast, the great Eastern religions think of time as an endless series of cycles, not heading in a particular direction. This seems to make any kind of strategy a transitory and evanescent feature of the world, a work of kings and leaders and generals who will disappear from the scene and leave no permanent mark on the shape of existence. Nothing is utterly irreversible. Whereas for Christianity everything in the world is forever different after the coming of Christ, as for Judaism everything is different after the giving of the Torah to Moses and for Muslims everything is different after the revealing of the Qur'an.

So the monotheist religions share a distinctive metaphysics of time, one more hospitable than the Eastern religions to the notion that the world itself and its history may be given shape by a divine strategy, which results in a particular story with its unique characters, its unrepeatable events, and its direction toward a definite (though only partly discernible) *dénouement*. We have here a metaphysics with room, as it were, for an ultimate strategy.

2. *Philosophy.* All three monotheist religions have had some kind of relation with the Greek philosophical tradition. The great question of that tradition, as identified by the Christian thinker Augustine, is "What is happiness?" where happiness is understood not simply as a moment of pleasure or contentment but as the true and lasting success of a human life. The great assumption of the philosophical tradition, as Augustine identified it (following Cicero's *Hortensius*, who was following Aristotle's *Protrepticus*, who was following Plato's *Euthydemus*) is "We all desire to be happy." The monotheist religions all offered an answer to this question about happiness, and a road to the fulfillment of this desire (in contrast, say, to Buddhism, which had a different question, because it aimed at the cessation of desire rather than its fulfillment).

Yet the goal of happiness is not yet a strategy. It is indeed far too vague. That is why the crucial question the philosophers had to answer concerned what happiness really is, and how to get there. But once one has defined happiness in some way, such as pleasure, wealth, honor, power, or wisdom, then one can begin to envisage a strategy for attaining it, a road that will get one to this goal.

And yet this too is not yet a strategy, if it is only the goal of an individual. Strategy concerns collective action, the direction taken by an organized group or community. By contrast, the philosophical schools that reached their mature form in the Hellenistic era were strikingly individualistic, holding up the life of the wise man as the paradigm of happiness. The road to happiness was the wisdom and virtue of an exemplary individual soul. Hence in ancient philosophical ethics we find a way of life and formation of the soul, perhaps even a method, but not a strategy.

But now we can take one further step with Augustine, who insists that happiness is social, a shared goal based on a common good. None of us can ultimately be happy alone, but only as members of a community, which Augustine calls the City of God. We are ultimately happy only by sharing with one another the ultimate Good, which Augustine of course identifies as God. He says that pagan Platonists actually agreed with Christians on this point, but they never hoped to bring a whole community (a whole city or *polis*) to this goal. That would require an authority, which in Augustine means a form of teaching, that the Platonists did not have. They could not conceive a way of teaching the crowd or "the many" (*hoi polloi*) the way to the happiness of knowing the supreme Good. Augustine argues that the apostles of Christ presented just such a way, an authority that has already succeeded in leading even the uneducated to virtue and wisdom and ultimately to happiness or beatitude. From this Augustinian perspective, Nietzsche was so not far off in the preface to *Beyond Good and Evil*, when he said Christianity represents "Platonism for the masses"!

3. Israel and the Nations. But I propose not to follow Augustine's interpretation of Christianity in all respects. This will have a great deal to do with how I understand God's strategy. Augustine divided the human race into two groups, the City of God and the Earthly City, the one destined for eternal happiness with God and the other destined for eternal destruction. Ultimately the difference between them is made by God's election, his choice to save some but not others. But I think the biblical story, shared by Christians and Jews, is not the story of these two cities. It *is* the story of divine election, carried out by divine strategy, but the two groups it envisions are Israel and the nations or (in New Testament terms) Jews and Gentiles. To understand the divine strategy represented in the story of the Bible is to understand how God chooses the one group, Israel, for the blessing of all others.

I would distinguish this way of reading the Biblical story from some more familiar readings. Augustine is useful as a very sophisticated representative of the latter. Augustine's division of humanity into two cities represents the conviction that the ultimate issue for humanity is, "Who shall be saved, and who shall be damned?" Another way to put it is: "Who gets

1 – A Strategy of Blessing?

to go to heaven?" A more Augustinian way of putting it is: who belongs to the City of God?

But in the Bible—and I am proposing, also in a proper Christian reading of the Bible—the most important division in humanity is between Israel and the nations, Jew and Gentile, and this is not at all equivalent to the division between the saved and the damned. In contrast to the Augustinian concept of election, in which God chooses *some for salvation but not others*, I think it is clear that the biblical concept of election portrays God as choosing *some for the blessing of others*. It was Karl Barth, the great twentieth-century Swiss theologian, who first convinced many Christians that the biblical concept of election presented us with this structure of blessing and good news for all, which is at the root of the strategy of God that I propose to explore with you. I take the work of Jesus Christ, the king of the Jews, to be the culmination, not the reversal, of the divine strategy found in the biblical concept of election.

So here is one familiar way of reading the Bible that I want to avoid: the idea that the Jews are a particular tribe concerned with their own security and survival, and what happens in the New Testament is that the monotheism of the Jews becomes universal, no longer tied to the ethnic identity of Israel but a religion for humanity as such. Here again I think Nietzsche got it right: Christianity is not a universal religion of reason, but an extension of Judaism by other means.[2] In Pauline terms, it is a way of bringing Gentiles into the covenant with Israel, like grafting wild branches onto a cultivated olive tree so that they may share its life (Rom 11:17–24).

In the view of much recent scholarship, Christianity began as a Jewish movement contending with other first-century Jewish movements about the true identity of Israel. That is what I think it still is. Gentile Christians are honorary Jews, adopted brothers and sisters of the children of Israel. That is the universalism of Christianity. It does not simply abolish the difference between Jew and Gentile, but sees it as a source of mutual blessing. How to carry out this project of blessing each through the other is the task of divine strategy, which has many obstacles to face since Jews and Gentiles

---

2. See Nietzsche, *Genealogy of Morals*, Essay 1, §8. Of course I don't accept Nietzsche's depiction of "Jewish hatred" as the source of "Christian love." But to be fair, his purpose in speaking this way was to ridicule the respectable anti-Semitism of his day, by undermining its chauvinistic assumption that Christian love was a novel historical development unlike anything in Judaism. God bless him, there was nothing he despised so much as German anti-Semitism, with its "Christian-Aryan-bourgeois" moralizing (ibid., Essay 3, §27).

Does God Have a Strategy?

are so apt to be at each others' throats. This is the context in which I propose to discuss the vexed issue of religious intolerance.

4. *Story and Strategy.* You suggest the Old Testament is like a movie, the New Testament like a snapshot. Allow me to change the analogy just a little. Think of the Old Testament as a huge novel, a story with many, many chapters, written in many installments, like the long nineteenth-century novels of authors like Dickens and Dostoevsky, who would write a new set of chapters every month for publication in a periodical. Now imagine that our periodical publishes a final chapter, or at least one that claims to be the final chapter. After a thousand pages, covering more than a thousand years, one chapter comes along, telling a story of a few years or even a few days, and claims to be the culmination of the whole story. This is the *coup de grâce*, which brings everything to its fulfillment! Or so the chapter itself says, calling itself in Greek the *eschaton* or the end.

So the New Testament presents itself as the story of the *eschaton*, the "last days" that have already begun to take place on the cross of Christ, and in his resurrection and exaltation at God's right hand (see Heb 1:1-2). For the New Testament, the end of the world is in a certain sense already behind us. Everything after this is epilogue. It is a surprisingly long epilogue, two millennia so far, and one of the essential tasks of the church is to interpret the meaning of this epilogue in which it exists. But it cannot do so rightly, more and more Christian theologians have come to think, except by seeing itself as belonging to the culmination, rather than the repudiation, of the election of Israel—and, we could add, the divine strategy that follows from that election.

One important set of questions arising from the incorporation of the story of the church into the biblical story of Israel has to do with the resulting *rules of action*, to use your terms. To discuss these we must begin with what the Old Testament calls Torah, literally "instruction," which refers both to the five books of Moses and the Law they contain. What to make of this Law, and how it is to be honored by Christians when many Christians turn out to be Gentiles, not Jews, is the crucial controversy addressed by Paul in the New Testament. What are the rules of action for those who follow Christ, which is to say the Messiah, the King of the Jews, when so many of his followers are not Jews but Gentiles? Jesus himself had a great deal to say that is pertinent on this point, since he also was an interpreter of the Jewish Law, very much concerned with the identity of the true Israel.

1 – A Strategy of Blessing?

Another important set of questions arises from the standpoint of leadership—concerning the chief or head. (I want to bear in mind that the French term for leader, *chef*, like the English "chief," comes ultimately from the Latin *caput*, meaning "head." Thus it connects with New Testament language for Christ, who is the head of the church, which is his body.) So we have a social body whose head is Christ or *Christos*, which is Greek for Messiah, the anointed successor of David as King of the Jews, who is now reigning at God's right hand as "firstborn from the dead" (Col 1:18). The church's strategy must ultimately flow from him. But of course it is reasonable to doubt that it always does, and this is bound to become a major issue in our discussion as we proceed. The church has its own history of murderous jealousy, as the Jews can attest. This does not mean it has no part in divine strategy, but rather that it is the most prominent among those recalcitrant others that divine strategy must deal with. As we have already noticed in the Old Testament, God is the kind of strategist who must constantly keep an eye on rebellion within the ranks.

One further issue that I will want to take up later is the metaphysical peculiarity of a concept of God in which he is both the source of all being and an agent within the story of the world—such that he must have a strategy to deal with recalcitrant others. The very idea that God has others to deal with is a little strange, but it is at the foundation of everything else.

2
Three Jealous Brothers

Jean-François Phelizon—It is only the monotheist religions—or rather, the Abrahamic ones—that essentially interest us. So I will set aside the others *a priori*.

1. To begin with, let us consider the Jewish and Christian religions. Whereas the Jewish religion appeared four or five thousand years ago and continues its history today, the Christian religions (at this stage of the discussion, let us conflate Catholicism and Protestantism) appeared two thousand years ago.

Now, let me explain that the Old Testament was composed gradually over the course of the first ten centuries of the existence of the Jewish people, while the New Testament is the quite *idealized* witness to the teachings of Christ, dating from the end of the first century or the beginning of the second century AD. The most widely accepted theory nowadays about the origin of the Gospels is the "two-source" theory, with *Matthew* and *Luke* being written using the Gospel of *Mark* and a source containing sayings of Jesus (these are called the "synoptic" Gospels). *John* comes from an independent tradition that is clearly much later and therefore less accurate.

What is interesting—always in relation to the possibility of a divine strategy—is these last two thousand years. Because these religions remain different (and in some respects "competitive") there seem to be two strategies present. Furthermore, there is no reason why the *end of history*, a concept characteristic of monotheist religions, should be the same for the

2 – Three Jealous Brothers

Jewish and Christian religions, since this end was written for the one before the other even existed.

More broadly, the search for individual happiness, for complete and lasting inner peace (Nirvana) is too vague to represent the end of history. In view of the collective aspect of all strategy, I am willing to admit that we are getting closer to the concept of a divine strategy when we talk about the search for a social happiness. Still, there is more to strategy than that. Because it takes on a collective aspect, thus opposing other communities, strategy must bring something to the group, to the community—most of the time to the detriment of competing communities. At the very least, this "something" is quite simply the survival of the community in question. All strategic action must result in securing the survival of the group: an agonistic group inevitably ends up disappearing if it has no strategy.

From this perspective, it seems to me there is a place for a divine strategy in the Jewish religion, because despite many vicissitudes it has secured its survival for five thousand years. Doesn't the Bible itself go in this direction? But this is less obvious for the Christian religion as it appears in the New Testament. To be sure, Christianity has also secured its survival for two thousand years, but as the New Testament is a "snapshot," a divine strategy is less evident. Would a divine strategy come to light if later texts, particularly those of Augustine and Aquinas, were added to the New Testament?

2. It is precisely on the relative value of the Bible that we need to come to an understanding. You say this sacred book is shared (and thus recognized) by Jews and Christians. This is true of the Old Testament, not the New. Christ is indeed "the King of the Jews," but only for Christians, not for Jews (and this from the beginning, as one can realize from the trial of Paul, in Acts 23). Thus the divine strategy, if we come to the conclusion that it does exist, must be considered in two respects: first in the Old Testament for the Jewish religion, then in the New Testament for the Christian religion.

More precisely, we are faced with two questions: is there a divine strategy in the Jewish religion? And is there a divine strategy in the Christian religion? *A priori,* one could perfectly well answer yes to the first question and no to the second (or conversely, no to the first and yes to the second). With regard to these two questions we need to resituate the Augustinian distinction. I would be tempted to say that in the Old Testament there is indeed a distinction between Jews and Gentiles—a distinction and even an opposition. On the other hand, in the New Testament, as extended by the writings of Augustine and many other Christian theologians, the distinction—or rather, the opposition—is no longer between Jews and Gentiles but, if I may put it this way, between damned Jews and Gentiles and saved Jews and Gentiles.

To posit that Christians are "honorary Jews," brothers and sisters adopted by the children of Israel, is a clever postulate that has the advantage of reconciling everything: for then indeed it's all about the same God in the Old and New Testament, and history continues onward without a break between Israel and Christianity. But this postulate remains questionable, for a number of reasons. First of all, do the Jews actually agree? I don't think so. There's at least one other truth to take account of—theirs. And then, this ongoing history between the Old and New Testament is continued further with the Qur'an, which refers to it. Do Muslims too consider themselves "honorary Jews" or "honorary Christians"? Again, I don't think so.

3. I'm inclined to begin with a different assertion: the existence of a *discontinuity* between the Old and New Testaments, a discontinuity of the same nature as that between the New Testament and the Qur'an. I don't deny the filial relationship between the three religions, and perhaps it's in that sense that one can describe Christians as "honorary Jews." But a filial relationship does not exclude discontinuity (and vice versa, discontinuity can imply a filial relationship in some cases).

Looking at the possibility of a divine strategy through the texts of the Bible and the Qur'an, one finds that their messages are too much in opposition for any strategic continuity to emerge from them. The history of the Jewish, Christian, and Muslim religions is there to confirm this: as everyone knows, it consists of an unbroken series of oppositions, struggles, fratricides, and often extreme warfare. There has practically never been cooperation, real dialogue, or even mutual recognition among the three religions. *A fortiori,* there has never been continuity of thought or action.

4. The "leader" of the Jewish religion is God, the God of the Old Testament, who guides the people of Israel throughout their history up to the present day. The "leader" of Christianity is the *Trinity* and thus Christ, whose filial relationship with David is recounted in the New Testament but whom the Jewish religion does not acknowledge as God (quite the contrary, it considers him a false prophet). The "leader" of Islam is also God, the God who reveals the Qur'an to Muhammad, bearing in mind that Islam also does not acknowledge the divinity of Christ.

2 – Three Jealous Brothers

If the three religions do not worship the same God, then one has to admit:

— either a single God is pursuing different strategies with each of the three Abrahamic religions, and these strategies end up converging—which assumes the survival of the religions until the last day;

— or that there's only one divine strategy, but it has gone unrecognized until now by the believers of these religions, through lack of knowledge or recognition—a recognition or *"enlightenment"* that comes on the last day;

— or that there is no divine strategy at all, precisely because the religions are too different and they will never converge.

It seems to me we will have to take a position with regard to these three hypotheses.

Phillip Cary—Nearly all your questions are, in my view, matters taken up by divine strategy. However, the questions you ask are many, and it may take some time to arrive at a satisfactory appreciation of them. I do not say "resolution," for I do not think I can answer all these questions. Since they are a matter of divine strategy, I think the answers to some of these questions must come from God, as history comes to its fulfillment, its *telos* or *eschaton*.

> **1.** *"Furthermore, there is no reason why the end of history, a concept characteristic of monotheist religions, should be the same for the Jewish and Christian religions, since this end was written for the one before the other even existed."*

Indeed, the end was already written by Jews before Christians existed. This Jewish writing is in fact what Christians from the beginning called Scripture, literally "the Writing" (*l'Écriture* in French). That is to say, when the New Testament speaks of "Scripture" it is referring to the sacred writings of the Jews, which Christians took to be their own. This is not surprising, because the first followers of Christ were Jews. But it continued to be the case when Christianity became a largely Gentile religion. As a result, we now have a community of mostly Gentile believers claiming the Jewish Scriptures as their own, and calling them the "Old Testament," which of course is not a Jewish term. This is part of what I mean by saying that Christians must think

Does God Have a Strategy?

of themselves as honorary Jews. If they are not honorary Jews, then they are usurpers, intruders in the Jewish story who have no place there.

They came into Jewish story by believing in the end of history, the *eschaton*, as taught by the Jewish Scriptures. Like good Jews, they believed that at the end of history Messiah would come (to call him "Christ" was simply to say "Messiah" in Greek) and would fulfill God's purposes for the world—carrying out the divine strategy, in our terms. What was new, of course, was their belief that the Messiah was Jesus, who had already come "in these last days" to accomplish the work of redemption. And part of the eschatological redemption they believed in, the fulfillment at the end of history, was precisely that Gentiles like themselves should come to believe in this King of the Jews (which is yet another way to say "Messiah") and be welcomed into his kingdom.

This does indeed have many implications for the strategies pursued by both Jews and Christians. For of course Jews today do not accept the Christian claim about the fulfillment of the Jewish story. And yet this claim is not arbitrary, but essential to Christianity. Either Christianity belongs to the fulfillment of the Jewish story or it is not true. So this is a life-and-death issue for Christian faith.

There is an important asymmetry here, which you have pointed out from several angles. I would put it this way: the Jews are essential to the identity of Christianity, but Christianity is not essential to the identity of the Jews. If Christianity is true, it is the true fulfillment of Judaism—and thus Judaism is indispensable to its meaning—but Judaism can be meaningful and true with or without Christians in existence. The upshot is that a strategy for dealing with the Jews is essential to the identity of Christianity, whereas a strategy for dealing with Christians is a matter of historical contingency for the Jews.

This is not to say that Christianity is a trivial problem for the Jews! Finding a way to deal with Christians has often enough been a matter of life and death for them—to move on to another point you raise. So although it is historically contingent, it is often an urgent and inescapable concern, an issue for any strategy of Jewish survival.

Christianity has been a danger to Jews, I think, in large part *because* its identity depends on them. To use a biblical metaphor (2 Cor 12:7), the Jews have been a irremovable thorn in the flesh of Christianity, and one dreadfully common Christian strategy for dealing with this is to try to destroy the thorn. Like Cain, Christians become murderous because the very

2 – Three Jealous Brothers

existence of this brother of theirs, the Jew, is an irritant, a threat to their self-understanding as the true fulfillment of the Jewish Scriptures—just as Abel was a threat to Cain's self-esteem precisely because Abel's worship was acceptable to God (Gen 4:3–5). Like Jacob, Christians have taken the blessing of God from their brother, but now must deal with the uncomfortable fact that this brother of theirs is still in existence. It has been easy for Christians, over the course of history, to wish that this brother be no more.

Jesus' parable of the Prodigal Son, as I discussed earlier, concludes with an invitation to renounce such murderousness for something vastly better: to "celebrate and be glad, for this brother of yours was dead, but now is alive" (Luke 15:32). This gives us the direction of divine strategy for both Jews and Gentiles; for both must learn to be glad that "The Lord's blessing is available only through the blessing of an other," as the theologian Kendall Soulen puts it.[1]

This celebration of mutual blessing is certainly a surprise. It means that not only are the Jews to be a blessing for the Gentiles, but Gentiles are to be a blessing to the Jews—precisely by believing in the Jewish Messiah, as Paul argues in Romans 11. But this surprise is not a revolution that overturns the divine strategy. It is more like an unexpected plot twist that leads to the happy ending you knew had to come, somehow, if the story you're in the middle of is to be a good story. It changes everything in the story, yet it fulfills the story rather than wrecking it. We could say: it is a surprising, even ironic tactic that seems at first to go in the opposite direction from the divine strategy (using Gentiles to bless the Jews—that's backwards!) but that turns out to be, in all its implausibility, the most glorious way for the strategy to succeed. Thus the gospel of Jesus Christ, which offers the Jewish Messiah to all nations, brings about the fulfillment of the promise given to Abraham in Genesis 12:3, which I used to define the divine strategy in our first chapter. The New Testament itself indicates this when Paul, quoting the words of the promise, says that by these words the Scripture "preached the Gospel beforehand to Abraham" (Gal 3:8).

Until we reach the happy ending to this story, however, Christians and Jews have to deal with each other as recalcitrant others, and God has to deal with them both. That is why I think there is only one divine strategy. God's strategy for Christians, which is his strategy for the world, must include a strategy concerning the Jews, both because the Jews are essential to Christian identity and because Christians have, in their rebellion against

---

1. Soulen, *God of Israel*, 117.

Does God Have a Strategy?

God, been so murderous toward the Jews. This divine strategy toward the Jews must include a concern for their continued survival, in keeping with God's covenant ever since Abraham. But more than that, it must involve the Jews being blessed by Gentiles, precisely because of the Gentiles' faith in the King of the Jews.

The divine strategy is therefore two-sided. Its objective is not only to bless the Gentiles through the Jews but also to bless the Jews through the Gentiles. The strategy for Christians thus includes the blessing of the Jews so that, as Paul writes to his Gentile Christian readers in Rome, "by the mercy shown to you they also may receive mercy" (Rom 11:31). To accomplish this God will have to bring it about that the murderous brother (by which I mean Christians) comes to rejoice that his brother, the Jew, is not dead but alive—thus accepting the invitation that concludes the parable of the Prodigal Son. God's strategy must therefore deal with precisely the kind of questions about the relation of Judaism and Christianity that you have just raised.

2. *"All strategic action must result in securing the survival of the group."*

Yes, this is a necessary, though not sufficient, condition of all strategy. In the covenant with Abraham, this means that God will curse "him who dishonors you" (Gen 12:3). Christians, in making themselves the enemies of the Jews, make themselves the enemies of God, with crucial consequences for divine strategy.

But of course survival is not sufficient. The curse serves the blessing. God keeps Israel in existence so that Israel may not just survive but be a blessing for all nations (again, Gen 12:3). Precisely that divine strategy is fulfilled in Christ and resisted by Christians who are murderous toward the Jews. I take this to be an essential complication with which the divine strategy must deal, for reasons I've already suggested in my references to Cain and Abel, as well as Jacob and Esau. The divine strategy is, *operationally*, the strategy of teaching jealous brothers to be a blessing to one another and to rejoice in one another's existence. That leads to the happiness that is the end of history, the *eschaton* that is already fulfilled in Christ but not yet visible to us.

3. *"Would a divine strategy come to light if later texts, particularly those of Augustine and Aquinas, were added to the New Testament?"*

2 – Three Jealous Brothers

Indeed, we have already been discussing what a divine strategy might look like beyond the Bible, because we have been talking about the Christian religion, and the Christian religion did not yet exist in the New Testament. The New Testament writers are all Jews presenting Jesus as the Christ, the King of the Jews, and contending with other Jews that this is the true Judaism. Of course they are also dealing with a surprising fact about recalcitrant others: Gentiles are coming to believe in the Jewish Messiah, Jesus. This was unexpected. One would have expected that the Jewish Messiah was for Jews. So what is to be done with these Gentile believers in the Jewish Messiah? Must they become Jews (by being circumcised) in order to be followers of Jesus, the King of the Jews? Christianity does not become a distinct religion until the answer to that question has changed everything.

Of course the answer is given in the New Testament. But the changes it brings about are beyond anything the New Testament writers wrote about. The New Testament answer is Paul's answer: Gentiles do not have to convert to Judaism and be circumcised in order to be followers of Christ. It is enough to believe in Christ and be baptized, which is Paul's famous doctrine of justification by faith. It is by virtue of this same faith in Christ that Gentile Christians like myself now regard the Jewish Scripture as our own (we call it "the Old Testament"), because in bearing witness to Christ, the Law and the Prophets speak also about all those who live in Christ by faith.

But what was not apparent in the New Testament was that belief in Christ would result in a religion different from that of the Jews. So in speaking of Christianity, we are necessarily speaking of something that takes place after the New Testament, though as a result of what is taught and narrated within the New Testament. The New Testament points to a divine strategy because it begins a story but does not complete it, and it awaits what God will do to bring that story—and with it the history of Israel and of all the nations—to its glorious end. Christian faith occupies the time in between: before the end, yet after the beginning narrated in the New Testament, when Christianity was still a Jewish religious movement, not yet a new religion.

To interpret the divine strategy narrated in the New Testament is thus inevitably to interpret what has happened as a result of that narration—a history that includes not only the founding of the church but its expansion throughout the world as a result of the crucial decision to admit Gentiles into this community without requiring them to become Jews.

Now I think I can answer the next series of questions rather quickly.

Does God Have a Strategy?

> **4.** "*Christ is indeed 'the King of the Jews,' but only for Christians, not for Jews.*"

This fact is an essential concern of divine strategy according to Paul, in the Letter to the Romans 9–11. If it was surprising that Gentiles believed in the King of the Jews, it was even more surprising that the Jews did not. The divine strategy must deal with these recalcitrant others—the Gentiles who believed in the King of the Jews and the Jews who did not.

> **5.** "*We are faced with two questions: Is there a divine strategy in the Jewish religion? And is there a divine strategy in the Christian religion?*"

In the Christian view I am proposing, the divine strategy seen in the Christian religion is not only the fulfillment of the strategy in the Jewish Scripture, but includes a strategy for dealing with the Jews' recalcitrant unbelief and the resulting Christian murderousness, which is the worst and most difficult recalcitrance of all.

> **6.** "*On the other hand, in the New Testament, as extended by the writings of Augustine and many other Christian theologians, the distinction—or rather, the opposition—is no longer between Jews and Gentiles but, if I may put it this way, between damned Jews and Gentiles and saved Jews and Gentiles.*"

Exactly so. This is why I disagree with Augustine. The proper continuation of the New Testament is different from what he thought.

> **7.** "*To posit that Christians are 'honorary Jews,' brothers and sisters adopted by the children of Israel, is a clever postulate that has the advantage of reconciling everything.*"

This "postulate" creates problems as well as solving them, for it is based on a more fundamental premise that has not gone uncontested. Gentile Christians can be honorary Jews only if it turns out to be true that Jesus is the King of the Jews, which the Jews do not believe. So from the Jewish perspective, Christians must be usurpers or intruders into the story of Israel, claiming the right to be brothers and then becoming murderous when the basis of that claim is not accepted. So this postulate helps generate many of the problems that the divine strategy must solve.

> **8.** "*First of all, do the Jews actually agree? I don't think so. There's at least one other truth to take account of—theirs.*"

2 – Three Jealous Brothers

Yes, exactly. God must take account of this! This is an example of what I meant by saying that your questions are matters that must be taken up by the divine strategy.

> **9.** "*And then, this ongoing history between the Old and New Testament is continued further with the Qur'an.*"

Yes. But once again we have an asymmetry. The Qur'an claims that its revelation to Muhammad the prophet is the culmination of all previous revelation and prophecy, which have heretofore been incomplete. But of course neither Jews nor Christians accept this claim. As a result, Judaism and Christianity are both essential to the identity of Islam, but not vice versa. Moses and Jesus are both mentioned frequently in the Qur'an, but of course Muhammad is not mentioned at all in the Bible.

> **10.** "*Looking at the possibility of a divine strategy through the texts of the Bible and the Qur'an, one finds that their messages are too much in opposition for any strategic continuity to emerge from them. The history of the Jewish, Christian, and Muslim religions is there to confirm this: as everyone knows, it consists of an unbroken series of oppositions, struggles, fratricides, and often extreme warfare.*"

Here we may disagree. Or rather, it is apparently my task to persuade you that these oppositions and struggles and even fratricides are precisely the concern of the divine strategy. Strategy is often about struggles and opposition, no? This is precisely the kind of thing I had in mind when I began our conversation by talking about "recalcitrant others."

I also think there is more to the story of these religions than *simply* opposition and struggle. The divine strategy sometimes succeeds in bringing about respect, even love between these difficult brothers. But you don't hear as much about this as you do about religious warfare, because it's so often a quiet kind of thing that doesn't make it into the history books.

> **11.** "*But a filial relationship does not exclude discontinuity.*"

For sure. To come back to my favored biblical metaphor, brothers do not necessarily live in harmony. They can be jealous and murderous. This is precisely what the divine strategy must overcome. And the strategy has clearly not completed its task yet.

> **12.** "*If the three religions do not worship the same God, then one has to admit either a single God is pursuing different strategies with each of the three Abrahamic religions . . . or that there's only one divine*

Does God Have a Strategy?

strategy, but it has gone unrecognized until now by the believers of these religions . . . or that there is no divine strategy at all, precisely because the religions are too different . . . ."

I believe there is only one God, the God of Abraham, and that all three of these religions aim to worship him, with more or less success. I am arguing for a version of the second hypothesis, because I think one God has only one overall strategy. But of course, since I am a Christian, I believe Christianity is telling the most accurate story about what that strategy is.

Jean-François Phelizon—This notion of asymmetry is worth a closer look. I'm referring to your affirmation (quite consistent with the fact that you prefer the second of the three preceding hypotheses): *"the Jews are essential to the identity of Christianity, but Christianity is not essential to the identity of the Jews. If Christianity is true, it is the true fulfillment of Judaism . . . but Judaism can be true with or without Christians in existence."* It may be so—but why not go a little further? Following up this line of reasoning, you'd also have to say: "If the Muslim religion is true, it is the fulfillment of Judaism and Christianity. But Judaism and Christianity can be true with or without Muslims in existence." And so on with every later religion that draws inspiration from the Bible (the Mormon religion, for example).

Now here I disagree. There certainly are filial relationships, historically speaking, among the Abrahamic religions, but we have to recognize that the three of them have assumed their independence. This means that just as the Muslim religion is no longer a tributary of the Catholic religion, so also the Catholic religion is no longer a tributary of the Jewish religion. Didn't you yourself write earlier: *"for Christianity everything in the world is forever different after the coming of Christ, as for Judaism everything is different after the giving of the Torah to Moses and for Muslims everything is different after the revealing of the Qur'an"*? So we must conclude that these three religions are independent, because otherwise we would have a kind of "progress" in the monotheist religions, one that clearly never ends. *In short, humanity would go from revelation to revelation.*

So although there is a filial relationship, there is also discontinuity. Furthermore, the discontinuity is what allows the Christian religion to exist as such and to call itself "true." Without the discontinuity, it would have had no more reason to be "true" than any other monotheist religion, such as Judaism. Henri Bergson put it well: "a religion which was still essentially national was replaced by a religion that could be made universal. A God

2 – Three Jealous Brothers

who was doubtless a contrast to all other gods by His justice as well as by His power, but Whose power was used for His people, and Whose justice was applied, above all, to His own subjects, was succeeded by a God of love, a God who loved all mankind."[2] And then there's the observation of Goethe that Christianity is more violently opposed to Judaism than to paganism.

So God must "deal with" Jews and Christians but also Muslims and believers in other religions—not to mention Deists and atheists, those extreme "recalcitrants." If there is a divine strategy for Christians, it must include a strategy concerning the Jews, but also Muslims and others. Under these conditions, this strategy can hardly be summed up as "blessing the Gentiles through the Jews." There are not just Jews and Gentiles, at least in the strict sense of the term, but Jews, Christians, Muslims, Mormons, and others. And the "recalcitrants" are not only the Jews but also Muslim, Mormons, etc., in short all the non-Jews from the beginning of humanity to its end.

However, if the survival of the Jews represents God's strategy for the Jews, as the survival of Christians or Muslims represents God's strategy for Christians and Muslims, *then there is more than one divine strategy*. Because of the discontinuities between the Abrahamic religions, God would be pursuing a different strategy with each of them—strategies that could end up converging on the last day (so it is the *first* of the preceding hypotheses that should be preferred).

Of course, survival does not define a strategy. It is a necessary but not sufficient condition of strategy, just as the existence of God is a necessary but not sufficient condition of the existence of a divine strategy. But "blessing the Gentiles through the Jews" does not seem to me any more capable of characterizing a divine strategy. For this implies that there is no discontinuity between the Jewish and Christian religions, while there is one between Christian, Muslim, and other religions. Why this difference? We're getting into a kind of discrimination here that a Muslim might be completely opposed to—and rightly so, I think.

It is true that in the New Testament there is no belief that the appearance of Christ as God "coming down" to earth would result in the rise of a new religion. But as I have pointed out, the Gospels are a kind of snapshot, a fourfold "witness" about a very short period of time. This period lays the foundation for a religion that develops "against"—that is to say, in opposition to—the Jewish religion. By the end of the second century AD,

---

2. Bergson, *Two Sources*, 228.

the discontinuity is unmistakable. Very quickly the Christian religion was defined, solidified, and established in an independent fashion, not just forgetting its filial relationship but even denying it. It took on a life of its own, independently of the religions that came before and after it.

As a matter of fact, the break between the early Christians and the Pharisees beginning in the 70s AD spread to all other Jewish groups in a process that seems to have been completed between 135 and 150. The differences between Christians and Pharisees crystallized essentially along two lines: Torah *observance* (for example circumcision and dietary laws) and Torah *interpretation* (essentially the messianic claims of Jesus). From the middle of the second century AD the break between Jews and Christians is definitive, and the dialogue between Judaism and Christianity would not be resumed until the middle of the twentieth century.

As you say, "*The New Testament points to a divine strategy because it begins a story but does not complete it, and it awaits what God will do to bring that story—and with it the history of Israel and of all the nations—to its glorious end.*" Finally, to privilege too much the tie between Christianity and Judaism seems to me a little like trying to put a stop to history. It overlooks what happened after the Catholic religion was established. I don't see how that can be right. In any case, this question of the discontinuity between the monotheist religions appears to me to be absolutely essential. Indirectly it is linked, as we have just seen, to the very notion of divine strategy.

Phillip Cary—There is certainly discontinuity as well as filial relationship between the three Abrahamic religions, Judaism, Christianity, and Islam, all of them understanding themselves to be, in some way, children of Abraham. But I shall focus on the filial relationship because I am mainly interested in the interdependence of the three. For it is interdependence that creates conflict and therefore the need for strategy.

The children of Abraham do not meet each other as if they belonged to three independent religions whose truth has nothing to do with the truth (or falsehood) of the others. Therefore the existence of these others, the survival of the people called Jews, Christians, or Muslims, may also affect the truth of these religions. This is particularly so in the case of Christianity, because of its unique dependence on the people of Israel. As a Christian theologian, I make a point of teaching Christians that Christianity cannot be true if the people of Israel ever ceases to exist, for Israel is God's beloved, his chosen people, through whom he blesses the nations. If Israel no longer

2 – Three Jealous Brothers

exists, then God has not kept his covenant—and a God who is unfaithful to his own covenant is a God that does not exist.

To teach this is, I think, a moral obligation for all Christian theologians, especially in the wake of the holocaust. Gentile Christians must learn what is quite evident in the New Testament—that they receive the blessing of God only through the people of Israel. That means it is good news for Christians that the Jews are the chosen people. In teaching this as a Christian theologian I believe I am serving the divine strategy of blessing.

Abstractly put—at a "conceptual" level—the divine strategy is that each learns to find the blessing of God in the other. Concretely—at an "operational" level—this means that Gentile Christians must learn that they are blessed only through God's chosen people, the Jews. But it also implies the converse, as taught by Paul in the letter to the Romans 11: that Gentile Christians are to be a blessing for the Jews. The facts of history, of course, suggest that Christians have often murdered Jews rather than blessing them. That is why, when I spoke of "recalcitrant others," I had Christians in mind above all. How is God to deal with such people? He has blessed them through the Jews and called them to be a blessing for the Jews, and now they have made themselves a curse for the Jews, his own people. Schooled by the New Testament, where the relation of Jew and Gentile is the fundamental division in humanity, I take this question to be central to the divine strategy and thus to human history.

So I insist on the dependence of Christianity on Judaism because without this dependence and the conflicts it generates, there is no divine strategy to speak of. Blessing the Gentiles through the Jews would be easy if the Gentiles were not so murderous. And *Christian* Gentiles, at least, are murderous toward the Jews mainly because they do not want to acknowledge their dependence on these others. Above all, they have not wanted to acknowledge that they receive the blessing of God only through these others, who are God's beloved. I don't think Jews will be safe from Christians until Christians learn to accept that it is good news that Jews, not Gentiles, are the chosen people.

It is different with Muslims, for reasons that have to do with the inner logic of Islam. (By the word "logic," I mean to point to consequences of the claim that something is *true*.) The Qur'an teaches that the revelation to Muhammad is the fulfillment of the revelation to Moses and the revelation to Jesus, both of whom are frequently honored as prophets within the Qur'an itself. But what the Qur'an says about the Torah revealed to Moses is very different from what the Jews actually believe the Torah to be, and likewise what it says about the gospel of Jesus is very different from what Christians actually believe the gospel to be.

With regard to Christianity, for example, Islam cannot accept the Christian belief that Jesus is the Son of God, for the Qur'an teaches very emphatically that Allah has no sons. So if Islam is true, then Christianity in its current orthodox form must surely be false. The doctrine of the Trinity is absolutely incompatible with the teaching of the Qur'an. The implication, made explicit by Muslim theology, is that Christians have misunderstood their own revelation, and that to recover it in its pure and original form they must turn to the revelation given to Muhammad. It follows that Christians can find the true fulfillment of the revelation to Jesus only by abandoning Christianity, as it currently exists, and becoming Muslims. In this way the inner logic of Islam is incompatible with the truth of Christianity.

By contrast, the inner logic of Christianity is not only compatible with the truth of Judaism but demands it. Christianity cannot be true if the Old Testament is not true, if Israel is not God's chosen people, if the written Torah is not God's law for Israel, and above all if the God of Jesus Christ is not the God of Israel. In short, the inner logic of Christianity demands that the Jews are right about the identity of God, whereas the inner logic of Islam demands that Christians (and Jews as well) are wrong, in many respects at least, about the identity of God.

The difference follows from the fact that the Jewish Scriptures, which Christians call the Old Testament, are incorporated into the Christian Bible, whereas the Jewish and Christian Scriptures are not incorporated into the Qur'an, but regarded by Muslims as corrupted texts, containing some of the revelation to Moses and Jesus but many illegitimate additions that falsify what God had originally revealed. Hence according to Islam it is Muslims, not Jews or Christians, who are the true followers of Moses and Jesus. By contrast Christians, for all their insistence that they understand the Old Testament better than the Jews, do not deny that Jews are truly followers of Moses and that the written Torah they obey really is the Law given them by God. For if the written Torah of Moses is not the true Torah, then Christianity is false.

There is more to be said about Christianity's dependence on Judaism and how this generates Christian violence against Jews. The fact that Christianity appropriates Jewish Scriptures and claims them as its own is very important here, I think. But for now let me conclude with a remark

2 – Three Jealous Brothers

about the position from which I speak about these matters. When I speak of Christianity, about what is essential to it or its inner logic, I do not speak as a scholar of religion but as a Christian theologian. That is to say, I do not simply describe this particular religion but teach it, as one who believes it is true. I teach it primarily to people who share my belief in its truth, but am happy to converse with others as well. But especially when I teach the faith to other Christians, my role as theologian means that I have definite responsibilities with regard to those forms of Christian teaching that I think lead to violence. It is my responsibility to repudiate such teaching and to persuade other Christians, to the best of my ability, that this is not true Christian teaching. Thus my role as theologian also means that when I speak of divine strategy, I am not merely observing what Christians think about it, but trying to serve that strategy by what I say.

Jean-François Phelizon—I'm going to pick up again on some of your affirmations, beginning with the last.

1. *"It is my responsibility to repudiate such teaching and to persuade other Christians, to the best of my ability, that this is not true Christian teaching. Thus my role as theologian also means that when I speak of divine strategy, I am not merely observing what Christians think about it, but trying to serve that strategy by what I say."*

What you're saying here clarifies your whole argument. It is fundamental to know whether one is located within a "belief" or outside of it, within a "doctrine" or outside of it. Whatever belief (or "faith") one might personally have (or not) is clearly not the question in our discussion. I respect your faith. But the doctrine is a bit different, inasmuch as the issue is how to answer to the question, "Does God have a strategy?" For if you *have* to answer yes, then the question is irrelevant. As far as I'm concerned, I have not yet answered this question in the affirmative, or more precisely I remain *for example* with the hypothesis that the divine strategy might become apparent on the last day, with the "reconciliation" of the monotheist religions, and that in the meantime it might remain totally differentiated.

2. *"It is interdependence that creates conflict and therefore the need for strategy."*

That is precisely the question. For it is not so much interdependence that creates the need for strategy as discontinuity. Strategy is a guideline; it is

Does God Have a Strategy?

also an agonistic group's quest for survival, and this cannot be obtained except in opposition to other groups. If the three monotheist religions were interdependent—as the fifty states of the United States can be, for example—they would not have experienced the incessant conflicts of the past twenty centuries. It is because these religions oppose one another, sometimes very violently, that they give the impression of responding to *different* divine strategies.

> "Christianity, because of its unique dependence on the people of Israel . . . cannot be true if the people of Israel ever ceases to exist, for Israel is God's beloved, his chosen people. . . . If Israel no longer exists, then God has not kept his covenant—and a God who is unfaithful to his own covenant is a God that does not exist."

I respect this assertion, but in my view it lacks proof. This unique "dependence" looks to me like a recent discovery, and I do not see why the message of Christ would be *false* if the people of Israel did not exist or had not existed. In other words, the message does not seem to me *contained* within the Old Testament. It is new in every respect, which makes it hard for Judaism to accept or, if you will, it is not included in the divine strategy for Judaism. If Judaism no longer existed, this would not keep a divine strategy from applying to the Christian religions when appropriate. The remarkable survival of Christianity through the first centuries of its existence (or of the Catholic religion after the Reformation) provides proof of this, should one be needed.

3. "*Gentile Christians must learn what is quite evident in the New Testament—that they receive the blessing of God only through the people of Israel. . . . When I spoke of 'recalcitrant others,' I had Christians in mind above all.*"

This affirmation is, if I may say so, more "American" than "European." I am quite aware of the importance the Old Testament for American Christians, Catholic or Protestant. I think the view of European Christians is rather different. They certainly respect the Old Testament and read from it, but they do not *celebrate* it. Very few texts of the Old Testament are read during Catholic religious services in Europe. For European Catholics, the "recalcitrants" are the Jews, Muslims, or practitioners of other religions. A Catholic never considers himself a recalcitrant. The history of evangelization confirms this, it seems to me. Until recently, the goal of missionaries was to

2 – Three Jealous Brothers

convert all the recalcitrants they met, whether African, Asian, Indian, etc., sometimes even by force.

> "So I insist on the dependence of Christianity on Judaism because without this dependence and the conflicts it generates, there is no divine strategy to speak of."

Dependence or simply filial relationship? You're moving too easily from the concept of *interdependence* to the concept of *dependence*. They're not the same thing. I'm not aware of the Pope feeling dependent on the Jewish religion. Furthermore, I say again that discontinuity is what generates conflict, not interdependence. On the other hand, it is true that dependence can generate conflict or, in the proper sense of the term, a *revolution*.

Revolution is undoubtedly the appropriate term. It seems to me that in relation to Judaism Christ's message of charity is revolutionary, something that turns the whole society *upside down*. That is why there has been and always will be conflict between the two religions. Historically one is the daughter of the other, but at bottom the one is not reducible to the other; they are not *compatible*. How could they be, when Christ is none other than God for the one, whereas he is a false prophet for the other? However, this does not mean there is no divine strategy in the one as in the other. So the question is knowing whether these strategies are coherent between them or not.

4. Now for some quick comments on other assertions of yours.

> "Christians [should] learn to accept that it is good news that Jews, not Gentiles, are the chosen people."

I didn't learn that in my catechism class. In Europe at any rate, Christians are frequently told *ad nauseam* that they are "the salt of the earth." At the table where he invites the human race to be fed with his word and the bread of life, Jesus distinguishes his disciples by declaring that they are "the salt of the earth" and "the light of the world" (Matt 5:13–14). Which does not mean, of course, that the Jews are not the chosen people in the context of *their own* religion and doctrine.

> "What the Qur'an says about the Torah revealed to Moses is very different from what the Jews actually believe the Torah to be, and likewise what it says about the gospel of Jesus is very different from what Christians actually believe the gospel to be."

Does God Have a Strategy?

Yes, of course. The Qur'an is indeed located in this discontinuity. Muhammad too is a "revolutionary." He too has *turned things around*, and like his predecessors he has claimed to possess the truth.

> "With regard to Christianity, for example, Islam cannot accept the Christian belief that Jesus is the Son of God, for the Qur'an teaches very emphatically that Allah has no sons. . . . The doctrine of the Trinity is absolutely incompatible with the teaching of the Qur'an."

That in fact is the whole problem. The three monotheist religions stemming from Abraham have very different views of God. For Muslims God is one, Jesus is a prophet, and the Trinity does not exist. For Christians the Trinity exists and Christ is the Son of the Father. For Jews, Jesus is not even a prophet. As I said, this is *incompatibility*.

> "Christianity cannot be true if the Old Testament is not true, if Israel is not God's chosen people, if the written Torah is not God's law for Israel, and above all if the God of Jesus Christ is not the God of Israel."

Here again is an affirmation that I respect but that seems to me unproven. If the faith of Christians is "revolutionary" in relation to the Jews, this would mean that the two religions have different truths and that a discontinuity exists between them. Furthermore, if Jesus is the Son of God, this can only be for Christians. It does not seem to me that this would be shared by the Jews.

> "The difference follows from the fact that the Jewish Scriptures, which Christians call the Old Testament, are incorporated into the Christian Bible."

Here again I think we have a difference in perspective between Catholics and Protestants, and indeed between American and European Christians. In the US, the Old and New Testaments are one and the same book. In Europe, the difference is much clearer: Catholics are further removed from the Old Testament than Protestants. Perhaps this is the (unconscious) effect of the seventeenth-century wars of religion, which as you know in Europe turned into sheer barbarity. Might Protestants have wanted to mark themselves off from Catholics by a return to the sources?

> "Hence according Islam it is Muslims, not Jews or Christians, who are the true followers of Moses and Jesus. By contrast Christians, for all their insistence that they understand the Old Testament better than the Jews, do not deny that Jews are truly followers of Moses

2 – Three Jealous Brothers

and that the written Torah they obey really is the Law given them by God. For if the written Torah of Moses is not the true Torah, then Christianity is false."

For Muslims the Qur'an is by definition the only "true" book. For Christians the only thing that counts is the teachings of Christ (and the later texts which explain these teachings). For Jews, what Christians call the Old Testament is the only "true" book. One keeps finding this notion of incompatibility among the three monotheist religions, but I don't see why the Gospels wouldn't be "true" (for Christians, of course) if the Torah was "false"—nor why the Qur'an would not be a "true" book (for Muslims) if the Gospels or the Torah were "false." That these texts may obviously be "true" for those who believe and "false" for those who don't proves nothing about the unity of divine strategy, which is our topic.

Phillip Cary—I will certainly return to my argument that Christianity is dependent on the truth of the Old Testament. But first I think it is important to clarify some general questions about the concepts of filial relationship, dependence, and conflict. Then I will begin applying these concepts to the relations between the Abrahamic religions. Although the notion of revolution has its usefulness here, I will prefer the biblical metaphor of jealous brothers in conflict over their patrimony.

To begin with, let me distinguish three kinds of dependence. First is logical dependence, which concerns the concept of truth: X is true only if Y is true. Second is filial relationship, which has to do with origination: X would not have existed if Y had not given it birth. Third is dependence for survival: X cannot live without Y. I am proposing that logical dependence is an important source of religious conflict, and that a crucial remedy for this, at least in the case of Christians and Jews, is the recognition of the third kind of dependence: Christianity cannot survive without the people of Israel.

Let me now also distinguish dependence from interdependence more clearly than before. Interdependence can mean simply reciprocal dependence: X depends for its survival on Y and Y likewise depends on X. More often, however, it means that X and Y both depend for their survival on the same resource. And if the resource is scarce, then conflict is likely to result. This is surely a major cause of political conflict, no? It is also how *incompatibility*, another of our themes, generates conflicts. For if X's access to such a resource is incompatible with Y's, then conflict is very likely indeed.

Does God Have a Strategy?

My proposal here is that religious conflicts differ from political conflicts because of the distinctive role that truth claims—and therefore *logical* incompatibility as well as logical dependence—play in the constitution of religions. A religion's identity is defined by its truth claims, so that it does not survive if no one believes it is true. Therefore undermining a religion's claim to truth threatens its survival. But of course the survival of a religion is also threatened if those who believe in it are killed. Both ways of getting rid of a religion have been tried. But the *origin* of conflict between religions evidently lies in the incompatibility of truth claims. Because one religion's claim to truth can be logically incompatible with another's, the very existence of a particular religion—and thus the existence of those who believe in it—can be perceived as a mortal threat by members of another religion. The connection between a religion's truth and its survival thus becomes a distinctively religious source of conflict. And I think conflict is especially likely when, as I am arguing is the case with Christianity, one religion is logically dependent on something it shares with another religion, a common resource to which both lay claim—claims which may be logically incompatible.

Now you point to *revolution* as an example of how dependence can generate conflict. Indeed, this example seems to me to undermine your claim that discontinuity has more to do with generating conflicts than dependence. I think of the American Revolution, a conflict generated by America's dependence on England and resulting in American independence. Once that claim to independence was fully established and respected by England (which did not happen until after the War of 1812), there was no further cause of military conflict. Here we have a filial relationship between one country and its "mother country," which grew into a fundamental discontinuity between the two and *therefore* a cessation of conflict. Discontinuity, in the sense of freedom from dependence and from interdependence, means two countries have nothing to fight over.

So it seems to me that if the Christian "revolution" with respect to the people of Israel had been like the American revolution with respect to England, there would have been no religiously driven conflicts between Jews and Christians after the revolution was completed, as there is now no military conflict between the US and Britain. The difference between the two kinds of revolutions, I would say, is that there is interdependence between Christians and Jews in the sense that I have specified above: there is a Jewish resource on which Christianity is logically dependent for its truth

2 – Three Jealous Brothers

and therefore its survival, and its access to this resource appears to be logically incompatible with Judaism's access to it.

That resource is the Jewish Scriptures, which Christians call the Old Testament. The very fact that Christians give it this distinctive name, which Jews do not accept, points to a source of conflict, for it shows how important it is for Christianity to appropriate this resource despite Jewish objections. When Christians began calling this the "Old" Testament, they did not mean it was outdated. Rather, it was the ancient and original witness to Jesus Christ, from the very beginning of the life of Israel. So Christians and Jews agree that this Scripture is true, but they disagree about its meaning, about how it is to be interpreted and understood. Christians regard it as the ancient prophetic witness to Jesus Christ and Jews do not. This is a logical *incompatibility*, consisting of contradictory claims that cannot both be true.

This incompatibility is especially prone to generate conflict because there is also, for Christians, an essential matter of logical *dependence*: Christianity cannot be true if the Christian understanding of the Old Testament is not true. This is not because Christians must live by the laws of the Old Testament (although I agree that some American Protestants, especially the Puritans, have gone rather far in this direction) but because of what the New Testament itself says about Jesus Christ, which depends for its meaning and truth on the Old Testament. For instance, Jesus cannot be the Christ, which is to say the Messiah, the Son of David who is the king of Israel, unless what the Jewish Scriptures say about the meaning of David's kingship (e.g., in 2 Samuel 7 and Psalm 89:20–51) is true. Thus faith in Jesus Christ needs the patrimony of the Old Testament for its truth and survival. (If you read Pope Benedict XVI's books on Jesus, I think you will find he agrees with me on this point!)

Christianity and Judaism are thus interdependent, in the sense given above: they are both logically dependent on the same resource, the sacred Scriptures of Israel, for their very survival as religions. That this has actually been a source of Christian violence against Jews is something I think I can show you from the career of Martin Luther, who has a deep understanding of the dependence of Christian faith on the Old Testament, and whose theology has consequently posed a great danger to the Jews. The dependence that causes this danger runs deep, because it results from Christianity's very origin, its distinctive filial relationship with Judaism that, unlike its relationship with Islam, involves appropriating the Scriptures of its predecessor as its very own. If this is a filial relationship that originates from a revolution, then it is a revolution that has bred discontinuity but not independence.

Hence my suggestion for an alternative metaphor about filial relationship: what we have in Judaism and Christianity (and in a rather different way in Islam) are not mother and daughter religions, but older and younger brothers both claiming to be sons of Abraham and heirs of his patrimony. A daughter can outgrow her dependence on her mother when she reaches adulthood, but brothers who must live by the same patrimony are always interdependent, no matter how far apart they grow. So despite the real discontinuities, there is also the kind of interdependence that can easily generate conflict.

The metaphor of jealous brothers is biblical, but it is found outside the Bible as well. Most strikingly, Gotthold Lessing presents such a metaphor in the parable of the rings in his play, *Nathan the Wise*, which is perhaps the most famous Western proposal for a liberal pluralism in religion. Asked by the Sultan to explain whether God favors Islam, Christianity, or Judaism, Nathan the Jew tells this story. Three brothers all lay claim to their father's ring, which has the magical property that it will make its owner loved by both God and men. But having in moments of weakness and affection promised the ring to all three of his sons, whom he loves equally, the father finds himself in difficulties when he must decide who shall inherit it when he is gone. So he has two other rings made, each a perfect replica of the original so that no one, not even the artist nor the father himself, can tell the difference. And so each of his sons inherits a ring indistinguishable from the others. Now the sons can fight over who has the true ring—a question that no one can decide for them. But Nathan recommends instead that each should try to prove that he has the true ring by living in justice and kindness toward the others, so as to earn their heartfelt trust and love, thus showing that his ring is one that makes a person loved by both God and men.

Now there's a divine strategy for you! In many ways it is a lovely story, but it also paints a rather disreputable picture of the father, who makes promises he cannot keep except by a kind of fraud. The suggestion seems to be that each religion is not only equally true but equally false. The problem with this liberal pluralism, then, is that none of the three religions can accept it without renouncing their trust in their father and his truthfulness. Lessing was a great ironist, and I think his underlying conviction was that the best strategy for preventing religious conflict is to persuade all religions

2 – Three Jealous Brothers

to give up taking their own claims to truth too seriously. It is an ironist's strategy for promoting a fourth viewpoint, precisely that of modern liberalism, as the real truth.

In the end this does not seem to me to be a very hopeful strategy, because it does not treat any of the three religions of Abraham with real respect. We are not making much progress toward religious reconciliation when we ask believers to stop believing their own religion is true. I think Jesus' parable of jealous brothers is pointing to a different strategy, one that is less facile and more hopeful. The direction Jesus wants us to take is indicated in the conclusion of the parable, when the father tries to convince his older son—the faithful child who has a legitimate claim to the inheritance and therefore resents the extravagant blessing bestowed on his prodigal brother—that he too can join in celebrating that "this brother of yours" is alive, not dead (Luke 15:32). The underlying message seems to be that if you know you are the true heir of your father's patrimony, like Jacob rather than Esau, then you are probably the one who now needs to repent, for you are the one who is most likely to hate your brother and wish he were dead. It is as if to say: "O you who have the true faith! Can you not join your father in being glad that your brother is alive, not dead, and that he too is your father's beloved son?"

I read this parable, therefore, both forward and backwards. It looks back to the stories of jealous brothers in Genesis, but also forward to the future relation of Jews and Gentiles after the rise of Christianity. As a first step toward that future, it is an indispensable guide to reading Paul's great discourse in Romans, chapters 9–11, about the Jews who don't believe in Christ and the Gentiles who do, which revolves around the Old Testament passage, "Jacob have I loved and Esau have I hated" (Mal 1:2–3, quoted in Rom 9:13). Augustine read this as an announcement of who is saved and who is damned. But in light of Jesus' parable, I would read it as a warning that if we want to be like our father in heaven, we too need to love Jacob, which means we must aspire to be like Esau, the brother who is not the chosen one and yet ends up glad that his brother is alive, not dead (as we saw earlier in Genesis 33:4, the passage where Esau ran to Jacob, fell on his neck, and kissed him, just like the Father in Jesus' parable).

If I am right in my readings, then Christians are more likely than Jews to be the recalcitrant others with whom the divine strategy must deal. God is like a father who aims to make peace in his household by reconciling recalcitrant sons, and there is none more recalcitrant than the one who wishes his brother dead. And there are reasons peculiar to Christianity, with its logical dependence on the truth of the Jewish Scriptures, why Christians are prone to the wish that there were no more recalcitrant Jews in existence to challenge Christian claims to their shared patrimony. One way to make this wish come true is to convert the Jews to Christianity, and insist that this means they must give up being Jews. The other way is to kill them. Again, both methods have been tried. Christians have much to repent of in this.

My claim about divine strategy is based on the observation that neither method is what the New Testament has in mind when it speaks of Jews and Gentiles reconciled in the body of Christ (Eph 2:11–14). What the New Testament expects is that Jews who believe in Christ will of course *remain Jews*, just like Christ himself and all his apostles. The startling additional claim made by the Apostle Paul is that Gentiles too can become believers in Christ *while remaining Gentiles*, not converting to Judaism by being circumcised and observing the Law of Moses. So the divine strategy, according to Paul, is for Jews and Gentiles to be at peace with one another in Christ while remaining Jews and Gentiles. We have yet to see this strategy succeed. But of course Christian faith has always been eschatological, awaiting the final coming of the kingdom of God which is not yet.

In the meantime, I may perhaps ask you a question. I recall that you distinguish between external and internal strategies, the first concerned with the direction taken by a community in the face of opposition from others, and the second with the coherence and unity of the community itself. Since conflict and opposition can occur inside the social body as well as outside, I suppose there may not always be a clear contrast between the two kinds of strategy. (Is an elected leader who tries to put down a coup implementing an external strategy or internal strategy?) In any case, my question is: if God really is like a father trying to make peace in his household, then should we consider the divine strategy to be internal?

My thought is: from the Christian standpoint, Jews who do not believe in Christ are indeed recalcitrant others, antagonists who form an external opposition, but that cannot be how God looks at them. As Paul puts it, speaking again to Gentile Christians, "As regards the Gospel, they are enemies for your sake. But as regards election, they are beloved for the sake of their fathers" (Rom 11:28). The "fathers" here are Abraham, Isaac and Jacob, for whose sake Israel is the beloved child of God. So these recalcitrant others, who are "enemies for your sake," remain heirs, like the jealous older brother in Jesus' parable, to whom the father says: "child, you are always

2 – Three Jealous Brothers

with me, and all that is mine is yours" (Luke 15:31). They are antagonists of Christians, but children and heirs of God.

And yet—I cannot resist adding—that is not the end of the ironies in this parable. For the true heir, as everyone knows, is Jacob, Esau's *younger brother*. He is the one who, like the younger brother in the parable, made off with his brother's birthright and thus his father's patrimony (Gen 25:29-34), and then "took a journey into a far country" (as Jesus puts it in Luke 15:13) in order to escape his murderous brother (Gen 27:41-45). So which of the brothers in Jesus' parable really represents Jacob, the true heir and chosen one, and which represents Esau? It is hard to say—and this is part of the point, for Jesus is an extremely subtle storyteller, and a greater ironist than Lessing. There are puzzles here that I find deeper and more interesting than the facile impossibility of telling who has the original ring in Lessing's parable.

In any case, it does seem at first glance that Christian strategies for dealing with others, which are external strategies, cannot be the same thing as God's strategy, which is at least in part internal—an attempt to bring peace to his own family, as it were. For within his household he has more than one beloved and recalcitrant son living in conflict, claiming to be the true heir.

3

Religions and Revolutions

Jean-François Phelizon—There are two sorts of revolutions, or rather the word *revolution* is applied to two sorts of situations. The first is when brothers become enemies because the one no longer accepts being subject to the other. The revolutions in the New World are of this type. The subjection of American colonies to Britain, of descendents of the conquistadors to Spain, of Brazilians to Portugal, had become all the more unbearable in being linked to unjust taxes imposed by the mother countries. So people in the Americas rebelled in order to win a political independence that they lacked. Once independence was established and thus peace returned, there was nothing more to hinder cultural, economic, and eventually military ties from being reestablished. Jealous brothers, recalling their historic ties, started talking with each other again, if not collaborating. That is why ties between the US and the UK are so close nowadays. Faced with common enemies, and despite their geographic and cultural distance, the two countries had no hesitation in being military allies. This was the case, in particular, over the course of the two world wars in the twentieth century.

The second type of revolution is distinguished by its radicality. It consists in a complete overturning of values, where laws and beliefs are turned upside down, everything respectable *before* is no longer respectable *afterwards*, old beliefs seem suddenly obsolete, and the very foundations of society collapse. France experienced this kind of revolution in 1789. Ten years later scarcely anything was left of the France of Louis XVI. Russia too experienced this kind of revolution in 1918, and China in 1949. Here

3 – Religions and Revolutions

there are no jealous brothers being reconciled after settling their quarrel. The revolution comes to overthrow the social structure and society itself, and is furthermore usually imposed by force. The old society gives birth to another, which is radically different, and a return to the *status quo ante* is impossible; a point of no return has been reached.

What about the Old Testament and the New Testament? Judaism and Christianity? Christianity and Islam? There is indeed "revolution" but it seems to me that for you, the transition from Judaism to Christianity is a revolution of the first type, which is to say an inevitably short-lived quarrel between two brothers who used to love one another and are well on their way to reconciliation, while between Christianity and Islam it's a radical revolution, one of the second type. My interpretation is different. I think that between the three monotheist religions stemming from Abraham (to which perhaps we should add Mormonism and the Baha'i religion, which arose in the mid-nineteenth century in Persia), there have been changes that are radical and irreversible, and that these religions have implemented different morals, different beliefs, and different views of God.

Thus "an eye for an eye, a tooth for a tooth" (Exod 12:23–25) is a postulate of retributive justice characteristic of the Jewish religion, according to which everyone should be punished in proportion to the evil they have done. It's a matter of providing a kind of justification for just vengeance. There's nothing of this sort in the Catholic religion, for which a chief postulate is, on the contrary, "If anyone slaps you on the right cheek, turn to him the other also" (Matt 5:38). With this precept Jesus radically *reverses* the Jewish postulate; he presents Christianity as a religion of altruism and charity by contrast with the Jewish religion of commandment and law. Likewise, when Islam describes all non-Muslims as "infidels," it turns a radical new page, since it does not even acknowledge the *legitimacy* of the religions from which it nevertheless originated. Let us recall the Qur'an: "Surely they disbelieve [i.e., are infidels] who say: Allah is the Messiah, the son of Mary. The Messiah himself said: O Children of Israel, worship Allah, my Lord and your Lord. Lo! Whoso ascribeth partners unto Allah, for him Allah hath forbidden paradise. His abode is the Fire. For evil-doers there will be no helpers. They surely disbelieve who say: Lo! Allah is the third of three; when there is no God save the one God. If they desist not from so saying a painful doom will fall on those of them who disbelieve" (5:72–73). In both cases I think we are looking at revolutions of the second type.

Does God Have a Strategy?

But Christians themselves have experienced other kinds of revolutions. Protestants rebelled against Catholics in fealty to Rome and the fighting that resulted—so fratricidal!—can be assimilated to revolutions of the first type, *endogenous* revolutions in which two peoples who are like brothers come to blows, all the more violently and brutally for being closely related and in fact having too much in common. In this sense the Catholic religion would perhaps not have survived without the Reformation. To be sure, the radicality of revolutions of the "second type," which are by contrast *exogenous*, does not keep the people who unleash them from conserving part of their cultural "patrimony." After the French Revolution people still read Molière. Likewise, all the Abrahamic religions have a common reference point in Abraham, who is a fundamental figure in the history of the Semitic peoples. Abraham is considered the ancestor of the Hebrew and Arab peoples. He is also the father of Judaism, a patriarch in Christianity, and a prophet of Islam. But that doesn't mean these religions couldn't survive without each other, and in particular that Christianity couldn't survive without Judaism. They have clearly acquired autonomy in relation to one another.

Besides, what does this common reference point of the Abrahamic religions consist in? The Bible tells how the descendants of Noah, who along with his family was the sole survivor of the wrath of God, strayed again into paganism. But it happens that one of them, Abraham, rediscovers faith. Since Abraham is a model of sincerity and good will, God establishes a covenant with him, including circumcision as a ritual act of submission to be perpetuated from generation to generation. "This is my covenant, which you shall keep, between me and you and your offspring after you: Every male among you shall be circumcised. You shall be circumcised in the flesh of your foreskins, and it shall be a sign of the covenant between me and you. He who is eight days old among you shall be circumcised. Every male throughout your generations . . ." (Gen 17:10–12). Obviously the common reference point for the three Abrahamic religions is not this covenant instituted between God and Abraham, marked by its ritual of submission. It is simply the proposition that every virtuous person has to have faith in God.

Moreover, it is easy to show that these religions are different in nature, not just in degree. Contrary to the Jews, Christians find God in the person of Christ. They reconcile the divinity of Christ with the requirement of monotheism mentioned in the ten commandments by means of the dogma of the *Trinity*, according to which there is one God in three persons (Father, Son, and Holy Spirit). In this way Christians radically separate themselves

3 – Religions and Revolutions

from their original Judaism. For them, as you have put it, "Christianity is the fulfillment of Judaism." Muslims and Jews, on the contrary, see in the dogma of the Trinity a very serious distortion of monotheism. It is because the nature of the faith defended by the three religions is different that there is a breach between them.

And where is the divine strategy in all this? It can be located in the human context of non-determinism. By definition, we humans are free. We are free to believe what we want. Our faith is not determined in advance. We can "resist" for as long as we want. The coexistence of the three Abrahamic religions is a kind of illustration of this fundamental freedom. By leaving them free to develop each in their own way, each one "having a life of its own," and by guiding each of them in the direction they have taken under various human impulses, God accepts them as they are. Perhaps he accepts their independence because he has a secret strategy that he has not unveiled, which consists of maintaining or promoting them until the last day—while watching out that the faithful of each religion don't exterminate each other.

One can hope that eternal peace will be established in the end, that all believers will recognize that their divergences were only apparent, and that then the three religions will be reconciled. But meanwhile they are developing their own strategies, which must not always have God's approval because they bear the mark of human ambitions. These strategies are based less on respect for the "recalcitrant," on reconciliation with the *other*, than on the will to expand, the defense of their own teaching, and intolerance in regard to the faith of others. Sometimes they even seem to thwart the divine strategy, but it turns out God tolerates and perhaps even encourages them.

Phillip Cary—Your last paragraph evidently proposes a divine strategy very much like that in Lessing's parable: the strategy of a God who relates equally to all three religions, which is to say, a God who is not the God of any one of these religions—so that none of their strategies can count as God's strategy. Of course all three of the religions disagree with this point of view. And my disagreement with you, in any case, is very much like my disagreement with Lessing: his liberal pluralism imagines a religious knowledge independent of the three Abrahamic religions, with no grounding in any of them, which is to say, no historical grounding in the identity of a people who know God. Like the Deists, Lessing could call this religious knowledge

Does God Have a Strategy?

by the name "natural religion," as opposed to "revealed religion," and claim that the ground of natural religion is reason alone.

But such ahistorical conceptions of reason do not convince me. It seems to me on the contrary that reason itself has a history, and in the West that history produced Deism and "natural religion," which is in fact a very watered-down form of Christian monotheism, a distinctively Western phenomenon, not a universal religion of reason (it certainly does not look like "natural religion" to a Buddhist or Taoist). Likewise, Western reason has produced the philosophy of liberal pluralism in religion by appropriating some of the patrimony of Judaism and Christianity, including their monotheism and their ethic of love. Thus the liberal view of religion is not a neutral party adjudicating the claims of the three descendants of Abraham but a fourth jealous brother, dependent in its own way on the same contested patrimony as the others. The very fact that I disagree with you means that I want to draw you into this fraternity rather than leave you outside it.

Perhaps we will need to discuss the filial relationships of that fourth brother eventually. But for now, let us continue our very interesting disagreement about the first three. Using a notion dear to the modern West, you think of Christianity and Islam as originating in *revolutions* that make a radical break with the past. There is also, you suggest, a less radical, "endogenous" type of revolution exemplified by wars of independence. A fundamental change of laws seems to be the crucial mark of the more radical kind of revolution, though it involves changes in beliefs and values and social structure as well. So you apply this notion not only to political revolutions but also to social and cultural change, and even to religious transformations.

Once the term is extended so far, however, I wonder if the distinction between exogenous and endogenous revolutions can be sustained. Are all social and cultural revolutions exogenous? Or should we say that there are many profound sorts of social change that do not arise from revolutions at all? I am thinking of colonial America, which had a very different social order from England even before the American War of Independence—a social order without a landed aristocracy, for instance, and without a national church. This made it quite a different social order already from anything in Europe, and in that respect at least, already more different from its mother country than, say, Bourbon France was from prerevolutionary France. And all this without a revolution! Or would you say there was an (exogenous?) social revolution in America before the (endogenous) political revolution

3 – Religions and Revolutions

that began in 1776? I am not sure how useful the concept of revolution is here.

However, if I have to make a choice, I would say that both Islam and Christianity arise from endogenous revolutions, more like wars of independence than like radical revolutions. That does not mean, in my view, that no radical changes are brought about by these two revolutions. But I would look for the crucial mark of radical change in stories rather than laws, for it is in the stories people tell about themselves that they establish, assert and negotiate their identity as a people. That is why I keep coming back to biblical stories about jealous brothers, including the crucial story about Esau and his conflict with Jacob, to whom God gave the new name Israel. Christians tell the story of Israel differently from the way Jews tell it, but it is essential to Christian identity to tell the story of Israel—both of the biblical Jacob and of the people who descend from him and his twelve sons—and to find themselves within this story. In telling it as their own story, Christians lay claim to the patrimony of the Jews (who are named after Judah, one of Jacob's sons), even though the vast majority of Christians have, since the third century, been Gentiles.

That is a change more radical, in some ways at least, than the French Revolution. After 1789, it is still the French who are reading Molière as one of their own. The rest of us read him as a representative of *another people's* culture. But after about 200 AD, there is a large body of almost entirely Gentile believers who gather in worship to read the stories of the Jewish Scriptures as if they applied to Gentiles who believe in Jesus, and to chant the Psalms of Israel as if the God they addressed is *their own* God. When they read "whoever shall call upon the name of the LORD [*YHWH*] shall be saved" (Joel 2:32) or prayed, "The LORD is my shepherd" (Psalm 23:1), they took this to mean the Lord Jesus (see Rom 10:9–13), thus assigning the sacred name of the God of Israel to this man whom they worshiped as Lord.

So it is to this day. The identity of the Christian people depends on a radical retelling of the story *of Israel*, whose God Christians persist in worshiping as their own, using the same sacred text as the people of Israel, and identifying themselves as the people of this God, whom Jesus teaches them to call "our Father." They worship the God of Israel as "the Father of our Lord Jesus Christ" (e.g., 2 Cor 1:3, Eph 1:3, 1 Pet 1:3), which of course gives rise to the distinctively Christian doctrine of the Trinity, precisely as an interpretation of the story of the God who entered into covenant with the people *of Israel*. The change is radical, but so is the logical dependence on Israel's patrimony—and thus the potential for conflict.

Islam's relationship with its older brothers' sacred texts is much less intimate, and therefore contains much less intrinsic potential for conflict. Yet they do claim the same patrimony. In the Qur'an, Christians and Jews are not simply infidels, but are "People of the Scripture." Over and over again, the Qur'an refers to the Torah of Moses and the gospel of Jesus, treating them as true revelations of Allah, confirmed and fulfilled in the revelation to the prophet Muhammad. But unlike the Mormons, who designate their new sacred text, the Book of Mormon, as "a third testament of Jesus Christ," the Muslims do not actually appropriate the Old Testament and the New Testament as their own sacred texts. They see the Old and New Testaments as corrupted versions of the earlier revelation to Moses and Jesus, which is now more clearly presented in the revelation of the Qur'an to Muhammad. So reading the Old and New Testaments forms no part of Muslim piety, quite in contrast to Christian piety, in which the Old Testament is read devoutly as sacred Scripture (think of the use of Psalms in prayer) and in contrast to Mormon piety, in which both prior testaments are read as Scripture. It is therefore no logical threat to Muslims if Christians point out that the New Testament contradicts the portrait of Jesus in the Qur'an; they do not hesitate to say that the New Testament is wrong when it differs from the Qur'an about the content of the gospel of Jesus. By contrast, Christians disagree with Jews about the meaning of the Old Testament but cannot simply say it is wrong. For if the Old Testament is wrong about God and his Messiah, then so were Jesus and Paul and all the New Testament writers.

This does not mean that Muslims make no claims on the Jewish and Christian patrimony. Quite the contrary, they claim Moses and Jesus as their own. They are the most honored prophets in the Qur'an after Muhammad (and mentioned by name far more often than he is), for they are his essential predecessors, receiving the same revelation as he does but in less clear and complete form. Thus the Qur'an requires Muslims to believe they understand Moses better than the Jews do, and Jesus better than the Christians do. They cannot give up such claims on the Jewish and Christian patrimony without giving up the Qur'an itself.

Islam is thus like the youngest of three brothers, who stakes out territory at some remove from his older brothers' land and claims that his territory has always been their father's true patrimony. As far as he is concerned, his brothers are mistaken to believe they inherited their land from their

3 – Religions and Revolutions

father, and thus he has no interest in taking it from them (i.e., he does not read their Scriptures and try to reinterpret them). His brothers, for their part, don't believe his claims and would rather hold on to the land they presently have (and thus seldom read *his* Scripture). There is no cause for conflict so long as they don't try to persuade him that he is mistaken about their father's patrimony.

This helps explain why in Islamic countries Jewish and Christian worship has always been tolerated (though subjected to various restrictions), but disrespect to Muhammad and his claim to be a prophet has typically been treated as a crime. In most of the history of Islam, conquered Christians could continue to worship the Trinity in their churches, but they had no right to say in public such things as: the Qur'an is wrong about Jesus because Muhammad was ignorant of the New Testament. What could not be tolerated was publicly delegitimizing Islam's claim to the patrimony of Jesus and Moses.

Christianity's relationship with its older brother, Judaism, is different. Christianity is like a stranger who comes to the ancient patrimony (the Jewish Scriptures) and claims it for his own because, he says, by virtue of his faith in the father he is now an adopted son. "I belong here," he tells his startled older brother, "for now I too am the heir of our father, and this place is as much mine as yours." It is the kind of claim that is likely to cause conflict.

What is happening in this scene? Has the older brother sold his birthright, like Esau (Gen 25:29–34)? Has the younger son, like Jacob, stolen his brother's blessing (Gen 27:1–41)? Shall God welcome him like a long lost son returning home, as in the parable of the Prodigal Son (Luke 15:11–32)? All of these biblical stories offer ways of thinking about the divine strategy for dealing with these two jealous brothers. The attempt to understand this strategy and to obey it is intrinsic to Christianity itself, already in the New Testament. For the Apostle Paul, when he addresses the question why so few Jews believe in Jesus the Messiah, begins by thinking of the meaning of the prophet's fearsome word, "Jacob have I loved and Esau have I hated" (Rom 9:13) and ends by speaking of Israel's (i.e., Jacob's!) jealousy and how it may yet save them (Rom 11:11–12).

This is why I cannot agree to let Lessing define the relation between the Abrahamic religions. It seems to me that Christianity is already, by its very essence as a faith in the Messiah of Israel, bound to obey a particular divine strategy for reconciling Jew and Gentile in Christ, and that the surprising advent of a third brother must be understood within the horizon of that same strategy. So from a Christian standpoint, a liberal pluralism cannot adjudicate the conflicts between these three brothers, but can only be encountered as a rival proposal about the nature of the divine strategy, in effect a fourth jealous brother.

But suppose now we turn from early Christians, worshiping Jesus as Lord, to Jesus himself. Nineteenth- and early twentieth-century biblical scholarship, under the influence of the "great man" theory of historical change prominent in thinkers as diverse as Hegel, Carlyle, and Weber, portrayed him as the founder of a new religion. But more recently Christian scholars like Bruce Chilton, often in collaboration with Jewish scholars like Jacob Neusner, have seen him as a Jew arguing with other Jews about the meaning of Jewish law. There is nothing more Jewish than this kind of argument over the patrimony of Moses; such arguments fill the Talmud, as well as being found throughout the Gospels.

In his arguments with other Jews, Jesus was not proposing a new religion but a new understanding of Jewish law and the identity of Israel, one of many such understandings in the first century AD. Others are found in the Pharisees, in the Jewish philosopher Philo of Alexandria, in the various Messianic figures known to us through the Jewish historian Josephus, and in the Qumran community that produced the Dead Sea Scrolls. In this context, Jesus and his followers represented one of several competing first-century Judaisms. It was in fact the only form of Judaism to survive beyond the second century apart from the Pharisaical tradition, which gave rise to the rabbinic Judaism of the Mishnah and the Talmud.

Jesus' emphasis on love was not a repudiation of Mosaic law but an interpretation of it. He found the key to the Law and the Prophets in two commandments in the Torah, "You shall love the Lord your God with all your heart and with all your soul and with all your mind" (Deut 6:5) and "Love your neighbor as yourself" (Lev 19:18). These were not new commandments but well-known legacies of the patrimony of Moses. Seeing them as the key to the whole Torah, so that they govern the interpretation of passages like "an eye for an eye" (Matt 5:38-41) was a new but not revolutionary proposal.

What was revolutionary was the centrality of Jesus' own person to his understanding of the meaning of Israel: his authority not just to teach the Torah but to issue binding interpretations of it on his own authority, and to present himself, his teaching, and the community of his followers as the fulfillment of the Law and the Prophets, the beginning of what he called

3 – Religions and Revolutions

"the kingdom of God." He appointed twelve apostles (all Jews, of course) corresponding to the twelve tribes of Israel, to represent the beginning of a new Israel over which God alone would rule in his coming kingdom. This was indeed a revolutionary threat to the priestly establishment at Jerusalem (another form of Judaism, centered on the temple and requiring collaboration with the Roman kingdom that controlled access to the temple) and it was enough to get him killed.

Then odd things happened. The followers of Jesus, led by these twelve, proclaimed that Jesus was not dead but exalted at the right hand of God (see Acts 2:32–33). And after several decades, this proclamation came to be believed by a large number of Gentiles. The New Testament clearly takes both of these odd developments to be outgrowths of divine strategy, though the latter may have been even more surprising to the early Christian community than the former. At any rate, it is the latter that made Christianity a new religion, but only after there was widespread acceptance of Paul's argument that Gentiles who believed in Christ should be admitted into the Christian community through baptism, without requiring them to be circumcised or to observe the law of Moses as Jews did. Paul's radical idea was that Gentiles could be grafted into the covenant with Israel, like wild branches into a domesticated olive tree (see Rom 11:16–24) without converting to Judaism, but simply by believing in Christ. That is the original meaning of his famous doctrine of justification by faith. Without this doctrine, Christianity would have remained a form of Judaism, because all who believed in Jesus would have been required to be or become Jews.

So the Pauline tradition, already in the New Testament, came to think of the body of Christ, which is to say the community of those who believe in Jesus, as embracing both Jew and Gentile, and thus as the site of ultimate reconciliation between Israel and the nations (see Eph 2:11–22). I take this to be central to the New Testament view of divine strategy. God aims to make friends of jealous brothers, like the father in Jesus' parable who invites his angry elder son to join him in rejoicing that "this brother of yours was dead and is alive" (Luke 15:32). As we can see from the later history of Christians and Jews, this strategy has had a great many obstacles to surmount. Indeed it is quite an act of faith to believe that such a strategy exists at all, given the history we know. But to believe that God has such a strategy is, so far as I can tell, absolutely essential to Christian faith.

Does God Have a Strategy?

Jean-François Phelizon—At this point in our discussion, it is worth pointing out some resemblances that exist between the three main Western monotheistic religions, in spite of the discontinuities that separate them. These twelve points of resemblance between the Jewish, Christian, and Islamic religions (there are certainly more) are just so many "proofs of filial relationship" between them:

1. Holy places mainly located in the Middle East. These holy places—at least considered such by the aforesaid religions—have existed for several thousand years. The holy places for Judaism are: Jerusalem (capital of the kingdom of Judah), Hebron (the traditional burial site of Abraham, Isaac, and Jacob), Tiberias (where the Palestinian Talmud was written down), and Sfat (a center of Kabbalistic study); for Christians: Jerusalem (city where Jesus was crucified), Bethlehem (birthplace of Jesus), Nazareth (hometown of Jesus), Antioch (at one time the center of the Christian world), and Rome (the "holy city" for Catholics); and for Islam: Mecca (site of the Ka'aba and the direction in which all Muslims pray), Medina (burial site of Muhammad), and Jerusalem (where Muhammad ascended to heaven to meet Allah). The various branches of Islam (Sunnis, Shiites, and to a lesser degree Sufis) recognize other holy cities of their own.

2. The concept of prayer, which is supposed to constitute a regular practice for all the faithful of the Abrahamic religions. It is an act of submission, indeed of a special relationship with God. In this sense, its nature does not really vary from one religion to another.

3. The rite of circumcision. Still practiced in the Jewish and Muslim religions, circumcision has been abandoned by Christians as a rite (however, it is currently practiced in the Anglo-Saxon world for medical reasons).

4. Fasting. This is found in all three religions (in the form of Yom Kippur, Lent, and Ramadan) and has the purpose of purifying the faithful, as food is thought to distract them from paying attention to God. The end of a fast is often the occasion for a feast (Easter for Christians, for example).

5. Almsgiving. This is one of the five "pillars" of Islam. Daily giving of the *zakat* (support for the poor) signifies that all things belong to God and that wealth is merely administered by human beings. Almsgiving is also important for the two other Abrahamic religions, where it reminds the faithful that wealth does not accompany them into the next life. "Give to the one

3 – Religions and Revolutions

who begs from you, and do not refuse the one who would borrow from you" (Matt 5:42).

6. The principle of marriage. This rules over sexual relations and procreation, in a basically monogamous sense (except for the Muslim religion, which allows a man to have four wives if he is in a position to support them). Correlated with the principle of marriage, the three religions codify procedures for divorce (although this is theoretically impossible in the Catholic religion).

7. Funerary practices. In every case, burial is recommended, in contrast to practices in other civilizations (for example, cremation in India). From this practice there clearly follows a certain form of relationship with the dead. For example, for Christians the dead are resurrected in the flesh.

8. The existence of places of worship (synagogues, churches or temples, mosques) where the faithful are regularly required to be present weekly (on Saturday, Sunday, or Friday, respectively). These places are administered by rabbis, priests, or imams who are to varying degrees representatives or mediators of God on earth.

9. Defense of a morality that includes notions of good and evil, sin (action against the law or established morality), prohibition, punishment, and reward. It is noteworthy that certain reprehensible actions are nonetheless "pardoned" if their purpose is to defend religion. It is thus that massacres could be absolved during the wars of religion in Europe.

10. Life after death. The Abrahamic religions claim there is a life that comes after death, in a "next world" that is more or less mythic. Over time this "next world" has been further specified: for example, as being a matter of hell, purgatory, and heaven in the Catholic religion.

11. Resurrection of the body. This confirms life after death, which is not lived in another body (as in the Oriental religions) but rather in the earthly body (although it is never specified whether or not this body, which lives forever, is going to be worn out by the wear and tear of its time on earth). One finds in the book of Daniel the first mention of the resurrection, but it is not a resurrection for all: "And many of those who sleep in the dust of the earth shall awake, some to everlasting life, and some to shame and everlasting contempt" (Dan 12:2). "The Saducees say there is that there is no resurrection, nor angels, nor spirit, but the Pharisees acknowledge them all" (Acts 23:8). In the Christian religion: "All who are in the tombs will hear his voice and come out, those who have done good to the resurrection of life, and those who have done evil to the resurrection of judgment" (John 5:28–29). As for Islam: "Then lo! after that ye surely die. Then lo! on the Day of Resurrection ye are raised again" (Qur'an 23:15–16).

12. The Last Judgment. Since this point of resemblance is particularly tied to the question of knowing whether or not God has a strategy, it is worth going into it in more depth. In the Jewish religion, the book of Daniel refers to the Last Judgment (*Yom HaDin*): "The court will sit in judgment, and his dominion shall be taken away, to be consumed and destroyed to the end" (Dan 7:26). Isaiah is more specific: "Behold, the Day of the LORD comes, cruel, with wrath and fierce anger, to make the land a desolation and to destroy its sinners from it" (Isa 13:9). Various allegorical accounts describe God seated on his throne, while the books containing the deeds of every human being are opened for "review," and everyone comes before him to have their actions assessed.

In the New Testament, the Last Judgment is extensively discussed. Thus we read: "The Day of the Lord will come like a thief, and then the heavens will pass away with a roar, and the elements will be burned and dissolved, and the earth and the works that are done on it will be burned up" (2 Pet 3:10). The Day of the Lord is described in the book of Revelation as the time when the dragon (i.e., Satan) will be thrown into the lake of fire with the Antichrist. On that day the earth will disappear and the human race will be judged: "Then I saw a great white throne and him who was seated on it. From his presence earth and heaven fled away, and no place was found for them. And I saw the dead, great and small, standing before the throne, and books were opened. Then another book was opened, which is the book of life. And the dead were judged by what was written in the books, according to what they had done" (Rev 20:11–12). There is no appealing this sentence. That is what led Augustine to say what you mentioned earlier: "I classify the human race into two branches . . . two cities, speaking allegorically. By two cities I mean two societies of human beings, one of which is predestined to reign with God for all eternity, the other doomed to undergo eternal punishment with the Devil."[1] The *Catechism of the Catholic Church* states that "When he comes at the end of time to judge the living and the dead, the

---

1. Augustine, *City of God*, 15:1.

3 – Religions and Revolutions

glorious Christ will reveal the secret disposition of hearts and will render to each man according to his works and according to his acceptance or refusal of grace."[2]

As for Islam, Judgment Day is described in detail in the chapter called *Al-Infitâr*:

> When the heaven is cleft asunder, when the planets are dispersed, when the seas are poured forth and the sepulchers are overturned, a soul will know what it hath sent before it and what left behind. O man! What hath made thee careless concerning thy Lord, the Bountiful? . . . Nay, but they deny the Judgment. Lo! There are above you guardians, generous and recording, who know all that ye do. Lo! the righteous verily will be in delight. And lo! the wicked verily will be in hell; they will burn therein on the Day of Judgment, and will not be absent thence. Ah, what will convey unto thee what the Day of Judgment is! Again, what will convey unto thee what the Day of Judgment is! A day on which no soul hath power at all for any other soul. The absolute command on that day is Allah's (Qur'an 82:1-19).

From these points of resemblance of the three Abrahamic religions one can draw a number of conclusions:

1. The three religions are formally close. What people do in their name varies considerably but in their manifestations they do not differ much from one another. The distance separating them from other religions, particularly oriental or polytheist ones, is quite large, but that which separates them from each other is small. That said, each of the Abrahamic religions claims to be *true*, contrary to the other two. Because they each possess *the* truth, they are in essence intolerant. This is the reason they are inherently in competition and fighting each other (and they have fought each other a great deal, historically speaking).

2. The Last Judgment is astonishingly similar in the three Abrahamic religions. It is the day when God truly displays his omnipotence by separating the good and the wicked. The former rejoice in his eternity, the latter are plunged into eternal tortures. But what are the criteria by which human beings are judged? Essentially *how much they conformed*, during their lifetime, to the precepts of the religion to which they belonged. This means for example that the Jews who conform to the precepts of the Jewish religion

---

2. *Catechism of the Catholic Church*, §682.

can be saved, but not if they convert and become Christians or Muslims. Likewise, there is no saint in the Catholic religion who did not die a Christian (belonging to the Christian religion is a *sine qua non* of beatification and canonization as a saint). And in the Muslim religion, infidels are normally damned unless it appears that they were converted to Islam before their death.

3. Exclusivity and thus intolerance characterize the history of the three Abrahamic religions. The first justification for the countless persecutions strewn throughout past centuries was that believers who did not conform (that is, to the religion of the persecutors) could be quite simply eliminated. So it is by coercion, *but in a good cause*, that these religions have ultimately succeeded in ruling over people's conscience.

This is where divine strategy comes into play, because it is in the name of God that believers practice exclusion and justify intolerance. Or else the divine strategy applies to all humanity—as I am inclined to affirm—and intolerance is a human invention, which is to say *an erroneous interpretation of God's will*. Or else the divine strategy is limited to a given religion—which I deny—but that implies that there are several Last Judgments and a great many people who are damned, because in every case, as we have just seen, God passes a severe judgment on those who not conform to *his* religion. *As a result, nothing prevents it from being the case in practice that an individual is simultaneously sainted by one religion and damned by another.*

4. What does Lessing say? He has left us indeed a famous parable (called "the parable of the ring") that is one of the key texts of Enlightenment philosophy and one of the most poignant expressions of the idea of tolerance. In the parable, the father represents God and the three sons represent the three Abrahamic religions. As the father loves his three sons equally, God loves the three religions equally—whereas they keep fighting among themselves, each claiming to possess the truth instead of imitating the love the father has shown them. Assuming the three rings are new, the father represents an original religion that is now lost, and the sons represent the three revealed religions, equally near and far from the primal truth. From this latter perspective the judge represents Reason, which enjoins human beings to devote themselves to educating their children rather than giving them the appalling example of their never-ending quarrels.

3 – Religions and Revolutions

5. If one thinks the divine strategy does not transcend the religions, then the Abrahamic religions—being quite competitive—could perfectly well disappear. In that case, every believer in a religion has a "right" to persecute believers in other religions *because he is right and they are wrong*. The Last Judgment will end up condemning almost all nonbelievers (and, additionally, all who believe the wrong things). Only the "good" believers, in particular those who have properly defended the "good" religion in their lifetime, have a chance to join *the God of that religion* in his eternity.

If on the contrary one thinks that God's strategy transcends the religions, then it comes back to what I wrote earlier: by allowing the religions to persist, "guiding each of them in the direction they have taken under various human impulses, God accepts them as they are. Perhaps he accepts their independence because he has a secret strategy that he has not unveiled, which consists of maintaining or promoting them until the last day—while watching out that the faithful of each religion don't exterminate each other." Then comes the final revelation.

In the first case, God is developing independent strategies and it is necessary to admit that the God of the Jews is not the same as that of the Muslims. God is to some extent the strategist of *his* religion. In the second case, God is developing only one strategy, not necessarily apparent to most mortals, but human beings may hope to comprehend it on the last day. God is in reality the strategist of all of humanity.

It seems to me that, in his immensity, God can't be anything but that: the strategist of the whole human race.

4
Truth, Tolerance, and Utopia

Phillip Cary—We may need to come back to some of your twelve points of resemblance. But for now I would like to focus on the problem of intolerance, or what I earlier called the "murderousness" of religions, which I illustrated especially by reference to Christian murderousness toward Jews. For as a Christian, it is the murderousness of my own tradition that I must reckon with first of all. I take this to be an obligation of all traditions, including even the liberal or Enlightenment tradition, which has some intolerance of its own to reckon with, such as recent French laws that do not tolerate distinctive religious clothing in public schools. It is a little too easy for all of us to point toward the intolerance of others. In the history of intolerance, this is one of the most common rationales to justify intolerance: *we* do not have to tolerate *their* intolerance!

I have already spoken of Christian murderousness and will again, because I think Christians are among those recalcitrant others for which God must have a strategy. But for now let me continue my recent efforts to draw you further into this fraternity of traditions that contend with one another about their mutual intolerance, by mentioning the trouble that Enlightenment liberalism has tolerating those it regards as intolerant. It is often said that liberalism can tolerate everything except intolerance. But that makes liberalism intolerant of every religion—if religions can only be tolerant by giving up their claims to truth.

If I'm not mistaken, your own presentation of the religions has now come around to the negative implication of Lessing's parable: if all three

4 – Truth, Tolerance, and Utopia

Abrahamic religions are equally true, then they all must be equally false. And thus I would suggest that in an important sense, for liberalism the moment of final revelation has already come. (You say "Then comes the final revelation," but it seems to me that the actual implication of your position is: "*Now* the final revelation has come.") For if what you say of the three Abrahamic religions is true ("because they each possess *the* truth, they are in essence intolerant"), then surely the truth is that their truth claims are all false. The result is that Western liberalism is a fourth tradition entering the same conflict as the others, claiming to know the truth that the others do not know about themselves.

Do you agree with me about this consequence? *If a religion's claim to truth makes it inherently intolerant, then its claim is not true.* I accept this consequence. That is to say, I think any religion that is inherently intolerant is necessarily based on false beliefs. But I also deny that Judaism, Christianity, or Islam is inherently intolerant. (I would like to say the same about liberalism and its claim to know the truth about the intolerance of the religions, but I invite you to speak for that.) My denial is premised on a more general point: it is not true that claims to truth are inherently intolerant. Let me first defend this general point, then look at the specific claims of the religions about such key issues as divine judgment, which will return us to the question of whether God has a strategy for all of humanity.

First, the general point. When two people disagree about what is true, the truth claim of the one necessarily implies that the truth claim of the other is false. But this does not necessarily imply intolerance. Think of how friends disagree. They are likely to state their disagreements far more bluntly, with less careful politeness, than people who do not know each other well, precisely because friends can trust each other. If you and I are friends, we can point out each other's errors and falsehoods quite vigorously, because we know that neither of us is trying to harm the other; we really are trying to find the truth together. And isn't that precisely what is happening in our present conversation?

So the question for me is whether the representatives of the various religions can learn to disagree like friends. The history of interfaith dialogue in the past fifty years has been very encouraging in this regard. My own experience has been encouraging as well. A few years ago I was invited to teach a course on modern philosophy in an orthodox Jewish university, and it was a lovely experience, even though we had plenty of disagreements to talk about. And it illustrated another important point about friendly

Does God Have a Strategy?

disagreements: they do not require everyone to meet on neutral ground, a space free of all imbalances of power. I was on their "home turf," as we say in English. I had far less authority in this place than my Jewish hosts did, but I was made welcome as an honored guest. Honest and respectful disagreements, therefore, do not require us to start from some neutral position, but rather to practice a kind of hospitality in the shared pursuit of truth.

Now back to Christian murderousness. For much of its history Christian Europe has failed egregiously to be hospitable to Jews. Only in recent centuries has it been safe for Jews to express their criticisms of Christianity in public. The friendly disagreements of interfaith dialogue are a new thing, and the question is: are they in fact consistent with the truth claims of Christianity—more consistent than the persecution they have replaced?

Obviously, I think the answer is yes. This is one of my convictions as a Christian theologian, but it is widely shared by other theologians more important than myself, such as the recent popes, the recent archbishops of Canterbury, and so on. It should hardly be surprising that such people would deny that Christian truth claims imply Christian intolerance. Yet logically, it *ought* to come as a surprise, if claiming to have the truth *necessarily* makes a religion intolerant. Or should we suspect that bishops and archbishops are necessarily dishonest, hiding their intolerance and their secret plans for persecution? That seems to me a very intolerant suspicion! So here I am proposing a vigorous disagreement with your liberal position on the matter.

What are the relevant Christian claims to truth vis-à-vis Judaism? They are, as I have argued, the claim that the God of Israel is the one true God, that Israel is the unique chosen people of the one true God, and that all nations are blessed through them. What is new about the way these claims are understood by Christian theologians today is the conviction that Israel *remains* the chosen people; it has not been replaced or superseded by the Christian church. This new rejection of "supercessionism," as it is called, is in my view a return to a proper Christian reading of the Old Testament as well as the New Testament.

This does not mean that Christianity and Judaism now agree on everything. It does mean, as I pointed out earlier, that Christian truth claims are logically dependent on the truth of Judaism. And I would underline again what I said before: it is not simply the disagreement between Christianity and Judaism that is a potential source of conflict, but the way that Christianity lays claim to the *truth* of Judaism as its own patrimony. Conflict can

4 – Truth, Tolerance, and Utopia

result not just from Christianity claiming that Judaism is false, but from Christianity claiming to understand the truth of Judaism better than the Jews do. This is not a unique or even unusual phenomenon. The Qur'an claims to reveal the true meaning of the Torah of Moses and the gospel of Jesus, better than Jews or Christians understand them. And Lessing's enlightenment liberalism claims to understand the moral status of the three religions (i.e., their intolerance) better than any of them.

In identifying the prime source of conflict among the three religions (indeed all four traditions, including liberalism) as their rival claims to the same patrimony, I am suggesting that the most offensive claim any one of them makes about the others is the way it affirms their *truth* and claims it for its own. To pick up an example from the first of your twelve points of resemblance, Jerusalem is a city over which there has been conflict between the three religions, but not Mecca. Why is that? It is because Christianity and Islam agree with the Jewish claim that Jerusalem is a sacred place, whereas Christianity and Judaism do not agree with the Islamic claim that Mecca is a sacred place. To use my metaphor: the two older brothers think the youngest brother's claim that Mecca belongs to their father's patrimony is *not true*, and therefore they have no reason to fight with him about it. But the two younger brothers agree with the oldest brother's claim that Jerusalem belongs to his father's patrimony—all three brothers believe it is *true*—and therefore they have fought for possession of the city many times over the centuries.

The same thing can be said about the father himself. Conflict arises between these religions not because they believe in different gods, but because they claim to believe in the same God. The Qur'an commands Muhammad to tell Muslims to make exactly this claim: "Say (O Muhammad): We believe in Allah and that which is revealed unto us, and that which was revealed unto Abraham and Ishmael and Isaac and Jacob and the tribes, and that which was vouchsafed unto Moses and Jesus and the Prophets from their Lord. We make no distinction between any of them, and unto Him we have surrendered" (Qur'an 3:84). But precisely the claim that all these prophets reveal the same truth about surrender to the same God, means that Islam, the religion whose name means "surrender," claims to have a better understanding of this truth than Jews and Christians. The next verse makes this clear: "And whoso seeketh a religion other than the Surrender [al-Islam], it will not be accepted from him, and he will be a

Does God Have a Strategy?

loser in the Hereafter." Thus for Islam, Judaism and Christianity are true precisely to the extent that their own prophets testify to the truth of Islam.

Claiming to understand another person's truth claims better than he does is much more offensive than simply disagreeing with his claims. And this is always what the younger brother says about his older brother: it is what Christianity says about Judaism, what Islam says about both Christianity and Judaism, and what the liberal Enlightenment says about all three. Since I think each must be responsible for his own offensive claims, let me return to Christian claims about Judaism.

There has never been any question in orthodox Christianity that the God of Israel, who made himself known to Moses, is the one true God. But then Christianity adds what rabbinic Judaism absolutely does not accept: that this same one God is the holy Trinity, Father, Son and Spirit, and that the Son is God incarnate, none other than Jesus of Nazareth—so that to worship this man Jesus is to worship the God of Israel. The crucial question to which Christian theologians have begun to give a new answer nowadays (but an answer that I believe is closer to the New Testament's view of things) is about what this means for the identity of Israel. Orthodox Christian theology has always agreed with the Old Testament that Israel is God's chosen people. But then Christianity, following the Apostle Paul, adds what rabbinic Judaism does not accept: that the true Israel includes not only the lineal descendants of Abraham, Isaac, and Jacob, but also all those who are Abraham's spiritual descendants by faith, "heirs according to the promise" (Gal 3:29) because they believe in the Old Testament promise of Christ's coming, which Abraham was the first to believe. Christianity is, as it were, a standing proposal to the people of Israel to understand its own identity in this radically new way.

What Christian theologians have recently come to see is that if this proposal is to have any chance of being true, it must be offered as good news and a blessing even for the lineal (fleshly) descendants of Israel. It must be good news for Jews *as Jews*. This means, to begin with, that Christians must reject supercessionism. The Christian church must not present itself as replacing or superseding carnal Israel, as if the fleshly descendants of Abraham, Isaac, and Jacob are no longer God's people. For the Christian claim on the patrimony of Israel cannot be true unless it is not only the fulfillment of Judaism but a blessing for the Jews themselves.

To get Christians to understand this is, in my reading of the New Testament, essential to the divine strategy. Christians must learn that their

4 – Truth, Tolerance, and Utopia

proper relation to these recalcitrant older brothers is to be a blessing for them. For Paul, it is an obvious truth of the Christian gospel that the blessing of Abraham is meant for all nations, just as Genesis 12:3 says, and that this blessing comes to the Gentiles in Jesus Christ (Gal 3:14). The really surprising point of divine strategy in Paul's theology comes in his discussion of recalcitrant, unbelieving Jews, where he implies that the reverse is also true. Not only are the Jews a blessing for the Gentiles, as the Old Testament has always taught, but now Gentile Christians are meant to be a blessing for the Jews, so that (as Paul writes to the Gentile Christians in Rome) "by the mercy shown to you, they also may receive mercy" (Rom 11:31).

If that is so, then the truth claims of Christianity, far from leading to intolerance, require Christianity to be a good thing for the Jews. The fact that it often has not been such a good thing for the Jews means that God must deal with Christians too as recalcitrant others who resist the divine strategy. Like the father in the story of the prodigal son, he wants *both* these brothers to live, not die, and indeed to be a blessing to one another.

This is why, early in our discussion, I suggested that the fundamental division in the human race according to the Bible is not between the saved and the damned, but between Jews and Gentiles. My point is that the division is meant to be a source of blessing and life, not curses and bloodshed. But the history known to us, including that told in the Bible itself, includes a great deal of curses and bloodshed. To believe that the Bible is telling us the truth is to believe that God has a strategy that takes these warring brothers from curses and bloodshed to blessing and life. It is to believe that God can make good his promise to Abraham in Genesis 12:3.

In the Bible, the Last Judgment is not the end of the story, for it serves this strategy of blessing. This is clear in the context of both passages you quote from the Old Testament. Your passage from Isaiah is one of many prophecies against the kingdom of Babylon (Isa 13:1–22), which are taken in the New Testament as a model for prophecies against the kingdom of Rome (Rev 18:1–24). Similarly, the passage you quote from the book of Daniel describes dominion being taken from the last of four mythic beasts, representing a final kingdom of evil, and given to "the people of the saints of the Most High" (Dan 7:27), represented by the Son of Man coming "on the clouds of heaven ... whose dominion is an everlasting dominion" (Dan 7:13–14). This was language very important to early Christians, who identified Jesus as the Son of Man coming on the clouds of heaven (Matt 26:64, Mark 13:62, etc.), whose kingdom shall have no end (Luke 1:33). The Last Judgment destroys

Does God Have a Strategy?

these evil kingdoms to usher in the everlasting kingdom of God, which is the central subject of Jesus' teaching and especially his parables.

Hence I would say that the kingdom of God, not the Last Judgment, is the best name for the direction of divine strategy. Throughout the Old Testament, divine judgment means the destruction of evil kingdoms, and thus the final judgment is the final destruction of every kingdom but the kingdom of God—hence the imagery of cosmic destruction, as if a whole decrepit and corrupted world were being burned up. But if the parable of the Prodigal Son is teaching us the truth, the kingdom ushered in by the Last Judgment is one in which jealous brothers must learn to rejoice that the brother they thought was dead is in fact alive. The recalcitrance that the father's strategy must overcome is the refusal to join in blessing the brother to whom the father gave away his inheritance and now the fatted calf (Luke 15:23). The Last Judgment serves this reconciliation and must not be understood apart from it. It belongs to the preaching of the good news of the kingdom of God.

Most fundamentally, the Last Judgment is not a strategy for punishing those who do not belong to the chosen people. If the liberal view of the intolerance of the religions were true, then we would expect divine judgment in the Bible to pursue a strategy of intolerance: it would mean salvation for Israel and destruction for the Gentiles. But that would defeat the purpose of God's strategy of blessing all nations, as announced to Abraham in Genesis 12:3. So what we actually see in the Bible is that the day of the Lord very often means judgment *against Israel*. See especially the book of Joel, where the day of the Lord brings a plague of locusts upon the land of Israel (in chapter 2), but "afterwards," the Lord says, "I will pour out my Spirit on all flesh" (Joel 2:28), which the New Testament quotes as a prophecy of the Pentecost, when the word of God is spoken in the languages *of all nations* (Acts 2:17). The chosen people are not the beneficiaries of a divine strategy that defeats all others, but rather have an irreplaceable role in the divine strategy that blesses all nations—a role that often entails great suffering for the chosen ones. On a Christian understanding, this is nowhere more evident than in the case of Jesus, the King of the Jews, who is *the* chosen one.

In the New Testament the judgment of God threatens everyone, because we all have our ties of collaboration with the evil kingdom. Hence Jesus' gospel is initially summarized as a word of warning to the chosen people: "Repent, for the kingdom of heaven is at hand" (Matt 4:17). So also when someone who called him "Lord" asked if many people would not be saved,

4 – Truth, Tolerance, and Utopia

Jesus gave his famous reply about the narrow gate which "you"—the people in his hearing—may find yourselves unable to enter, concluding that "some are last who will be first, and some are first who will be last" (Luke 13:22–30). From a biblical viewpoint, it is always *we,* not just *they,* who are threatened by divine judgment. Jesus' parables make this point repeatedly, putting believers in the position of those who need to repent. Thus the last judgment in the Bible does not simply mean: *we* get saved, and *they* don't. It means the gate to the everlasting kingdom is narrow, and all of us who seek it will find that what Paul calls the "old man" must die before we enter (Rom 6:6). The new man who results is not one who celebrates the destruction of his rivals, but one who rejoices that the brother he thought was dead is in fact alive.

In light of this hope for the kingdom of God, Christianity surely must reject the liberal Enlightenment claim that one religion's strategy cannot be the divine strategy for the whole world. Indeed, I do not see how any self-respecting religion could accept this claim. However, what is most distinctive about the Christian claim to truth, once supercessionism is rejected, is that the recalcitrant other, the older brother who remains outside the Christian faith, is nevertheless still the chosen people through whom this divine strategy of blessing for the whole world is made operational. For as Jesus explains to the Samaritan woman, "salvation is from the Jews" (John 4:22).

As the next few verses make clear, in saying this he does not deny his own role as savior, but ties it to his identity as the Messiah of the Jews (John 4:25-26). Hence we come to a result for which Lessing's form of Enlightenment does not prepare us: according to Christianity, the savior of the Gentiles is not a Gentile. He is a Jew, and he does not cease to be Jewish when he is raised from the dead and exalted to the throne of God—whence he shall come again in glory to judge the living and the dead, and his kingdom will have no end. It is thus an essential *Christian* claim that there is no blessing for the world apart from God's chosen people, the Jews.

Jean-François Phelizon—I find your argument somewhat reductive. For if God is pursuing a strategy, it seems to me it should be in his own image—which is to say, immense. It can hardly be reduced to merely "blessing the Gentiles." In general, it seems to me your assertions need to be sifted through the sieve of several contrasts: the contrast between history and theology, between sacred history and the history of humanity in general, and between the Christian world view and the world views of other Abrahamic religions.

Does God Have a Strategy?

1. Bergson said that while history is knowledge, religion is action. As you suggest, contemporary theology contrasts with the history of the last twenty centuries. I have no doubt that Christian theologians today are less exclusive than before, that they are even trying to reconcile the history of Christianity with that of the Jewish people. This development dates back to John Paul II, and even if the church of today appears a bit less energetic in this regard than twenty or thirty years ago, it is a fact that Christians of the twenty-first century are trying for a *rapprochement* with the Jews (not yet with Muslims). This has its contradictions, since in the past Christians never stopped opposing the Jews and vice versa.

Yet Christian ecumenical efforts could well be rooted in Christianity's relative loss of influence in the world, which correlates with the growing influence of Judaism and Islam. For it does have to be acknowledged: the presence of Christianity in general and of Christians in particular is declining. There are fewer priests, fewer of the faithful, fewer churches, fewer convents, and if Christian culture does remain present, it is hard pressed even in its strongholds by the two other Abrahamic religions, which are benefiting from a growing interest on the part of the younger generations. In most Western countries, the number of Christians converting to Judaism has never been higher. So also the void left in European and American suburbs by Christians is immediately filled by Muslim converts. I think we are witnessing a very important phenomenon: nowadays monotheist religiosity is increasing more among Jews and Muslims than Christians. In other words, fortune is not smiling so much on one of the "brothers" Lessing speaks of (who symbolize the Abrahamic religions, as we have seen) but the others are profiting.

I am far from thinking this change is planned. It results rather from the development of mores and of the "civilized" world in general; so we should take it all together. However, it must be emphasized that the ecumenical effort is essentially Christian—so the *rapprochement* is all in one direction. The rabbis and the imams are not asking themselves whether to try for a *rapprochement* with Christians. Whether they are moderates or extremists, Muslims and Jews continue to preach their religious certitudes, and if at best they look kindly upon Christian gestures of friendship, they are not taking any significant step in the direction of the Christian world—quite the opposite, I would even be tempted to say. Thus Christians sometimes say their God is the same as the God of the Jews and the Muslims. But

4 – Truth, Tolerance, and Utopia

for Jews and Muslims it is out of the question to *confuse* the God of the Christians with theirs.

Moreover, while Christians in the name of freedom of worship are allowing mosques and synagogues to multiply in their midst, there is no question of churches being built in Israel or Saudi Arabia. I don't blame the Israelis or the Saudis for this at all; as I said, I think a religion is by nature exclusive, that it normally leads to intolerance. The Jewish and Muslim attitude is thus in the strict sense "religious," if I can put it that way. Intolerance is an intrinsic feature of the Jewish and Muslim religions as it once was of the Catholic religion, back when it was in exclusive control of its territory.

In the past, Christians have had the same attitude as the Muslims and Jews of today. You yourself mentioned how often the Jews were cursed, persecuted, and exiled, if not exterminated, in the name of Christianity. As for Muslims, they did not live in countries traditionally under the sway of Christianity (in contrast to what is happening more and more today) but Christians kept fighting them as well as scorning them, from the Crusades to the wars of colonization. Thus over the 2,000 years in which Christianity has existed, one must count 1,950 years of exclusivity and intolerance and a mere 50 years when, following the lead of innovative and progressive theologians, the church has begun to accept a certain "relativism." This relativism, as interesting as it may be, runs counter to historic realities, and it is worth wondering how long it will last. It may be no more than the expression of a transitory doubt or the sudden awareness of a situation of unprecedented weakness.

So Catholic theology is developing, but the relative weight of Judaism and Islam is growing. This theological development is correlated with the diminishing influence of the Christian religions. I won't go so far as to say it is a result of it. But it certainly has resulted in the gradual disappearance of "the missionary spirit." What's the point of converting pagans or "heretics" if the difference between one religion and another is only relative?

2. The contrast between sacred history and the history of humanity is a realization of the nineteenth century. I have before my eyes a historical atlas (the *Synchronic and Universal Chart of the Life of the Nations*) that was published in Paris in 1865 by the abbé Augustin Michel—a learned man, judging by the profusion of details he has patiently collected. This atlas, a large folio volume that has clearly benefited from a very official *nihil obstat*, quite seriously fixes the date of the creation of the world in the year 3804 BC. The whole history of Israel is set down in detail here (for example, Moses came

Does God Have a Strategy?

down from Mt. Sinai in 1489 BC) along with that of other nations—at least those known to the author (who is unaware of the history of the Aztecs, the Incas, and the Chinese, for example). What has the abbé Michel done, in short? He has *reconstructed the history of humanity using the Bible,* and he has justified his undertaking by adding events from secular history (the birth of Alexander the Great, the accession of the principal kings, etc.) to make this reconstruction look credible.

This attempt to reconstruct the past still happens today. The Jews perpetuate this tradition. Thursday, September 29, 2011, all the synagogues resounded with the sound of the *shofar* announcing the beginning of the year 5772. But this reconstruction is not convincing. What could pass for *proven* a century and a half ago, the quite serious affirmation that the universe had been in existence for fewer than 6,000 years, is enough to raise a smile today, when we know the universe existed well before human beings appeared and will continue to exist long after they disappear. Under these conditions I think it's hard to reduce the divine strategy to the mere reconciliation of Jews and Christians. That really is too reductionist; the world is not limited to two Abrahamic religions, and the divine strategy probably has to be more universal and, if I may say so, more "subtle."

3. The Catholic point of view on the origin and destiny of the universe contrasts with that of other religions. Human beings do not in fact understand very well who they are or where they're going. They know that many things are beyond them (even more than they used to think), but they keep wondering about their own existence: What exactly are we doing in this world? And for how long? And for how much longer? The religions provide us with "explanations," to be sure, but they are not the same or consistent from one religion to another. If that were the case, maybe one could assimilate the divine strategy to a growing awareness among human beings of their place in the universe. Then all religions would be simultaneously "true" in that they would help the human race gain that awareness and "false" in that they would provide only one human response to transcendent questions.

I don't see why this awareness, which has accelerated a great deal since the abbé Michel published his atlas, could not lead us one day (the last day, probably) to the supreme revelation: the existence of God beyond all religious limitations. For this we as Christians have to get beyond the Oedipal drama of the Christian religion originating through separation from (and also to the detriment of) the Jewish religion.

4 – Truth, Tolerance, and Utopia

Let me mention in this respect the emperor Julian, who was a Neoplatonist rhetorician and philosopher as well as the last pagan emperor of Rome (361–363). The nephew of the emperor Constantine, he was raised Christian but apostatized, and hence came to be called "Julian the Apostate." Julian wrote works against Christianity and in favor of a philosophical paganism that treat the gods of classical mythology as allegories of higher realities. In one of his *Orations*, he said that every time the myths concerning divine truths present an incongruity of thought, they are crying out and testifying to us that we should not believe them literally, but should examine and investigate their hidden meaning. In this respect, incongruity is better than seriousness, which risks making the gods seem extremely beautiful, great, and good, whereas the use of incongruity allows the hope of looking beyond what is expressed in clear terms and rising up to the abstract essence of the gods, to pure thought transcending all that exists.

This supreme revelation has not yet taken place—far from it. It will coincide with the end of intolerance. So long as burkas are not allowed in Europe and convents in Saudi Arabia, one cannot speak of supreme revelation. With the end of intolerance, not only would Christians be able to keep claiming that the God of Israel is the true God and that all nations are blessed through him, but Muslims would stop wanting to impose themselves to the detriment of other religions, and Buddhists, Taoists, Mormons, all men and women of good will could discover one another, acknowledge one another, understand one another, and maybe even love one another. A utopia? Certainly. *But a utopia that only a divine strategy could have as an objective to attain.*

The truth is that divine strategy can only apply to the whole human race, from the beginning to the end of time. It surely did not begin fewer than 6,000 years ago and surely won't end tomorrow morning. So this absolute tolerance, whose coming we may all hope for one day, does not apply merely to Jews and Christians but to all the other religions that have ever existed or will exist. Today, the Bible is certainly the truth for Jews and also for many Christians, but it is not for Buddhists, Zoroastrians, Aztecs, and Egyptians. Maybe the kingdom of God is this: A world where human beings have no more need for religion, i.e., for rituals and priests and *intermediaries*, for God is infinitely present there. In this kingdom, the "recalcitrants" have disappeared, the recalcitrant Christians, Jews, Muslims, and all the others.

Does God Have a Strategy?

Could it not be that God's operational strategy is simply to let humanity prosper on the earth, and his conceptual strategy is to make them understand in the end the universe he has created?

Phillip Cary—We began with my endeavoring to answer your question, "Does God have a strategy?" Now we have come to your answer to the question. We have all along been making implicit comparisons between my answer to this question and yours, but now we can be more explicit. If you don't mind, I'd like to use the term *Utopia* as a label for the direction of divine strategy as you see it, while I retain the phrase *kingdom of God* for the direction of divine strategy as I see it.

There are some differences. Modernity's Utopia means tolerance for all religions, and yet it looks rather strikingly like the dissolution of all religions and their differences—as you put it, "*a world where human beings have no more need for religion.*" This Utopia seems to be universal by virtue of abolishing or outgrowing the rituals and priests and mediators that characterize particular religions. Whereas what I am looking for is a way of reconciliation that preserves particularities and differences, or what I would like to call *the otherness of the other*.

This is why I keep returning to recent efforts by Christians to affirm the Jews as Jews. This is also why I would not use the term "relativism" to describe the current atmosphere of interreligious dialogue. Relativism dissolves disagreements by supposing that each party has its own truth, which cannot really conflict with the truth of the other. But I think the other with whom I must be reconciled is one with whom I disagree, whose truth claims I do not accept. And even in the kingdom of God, I hope for a reconciliation that brings a measure of agreement without dissolving difference, so that I may embrace *another who remains other*.

Perhaps there is a sense in which this is a characteristically twenty-first-century hope, especially for Christians. This may well be connected with the secularization of Europe in interesting ways. The same nineteenth-century pope, Pius IX, who in 1870 lamented losing the Papal States (i.e., much of central Italy, which he had ruled up to then) as they became territories of a secular Italy, had earlier threatened legal penalties against anyone who opposed his "infallible" declaration of the doctrine of Mary's immaculate conception in 1854. He concluded his declaration by warning: "If some should presume to think in their hearts otherwise than we [i.e., the pope] have defined . . . they, by this very act, subject themselves to

4 – Truth, Tolerance, and Utopia

the penalties ordained by law, if, by word or writing, or any other external means, they dare to signify what they think in their hearts."[1] This kind of threat becomes far less easy to imagine when the pope controls no territory beyond Vatican City. In this regard the secularization of Christendom in Europe has been good for the Catholic Church and its practice of tolerance. But the point may be generalized, as for instance by the Christian theologian Stanley Hauerwas, who has been arguing for at least two decades that the loss of Christendom is good for Christianity. Christian faith may be better off without too much power.

In any case, whether Christians welcome it or not, secularization does seem to have advanced very far in Europe today. We will perhaps need to talk a little later about the vigorous spread of Christianity in places like Africa and China recently. But I should say now that in my experience, Jews and Muslims in America are quite eager to pursue interreligious dialogue. (And let me note in passing that, like other Christian theologians, I reserve the term "ecumenical" for dialogues among Christian groups and use the term "interreligious" to describe dialogues between Christians, Jews, Muslims, and other religions).

What is certainly true is that modern Europe (more than America) has become increasingly secularized, and that Muslims now fill much of the religious void left by empty churches. To think about what this secularization might mean for divine strategy, let me try saying something further about Western modernity, that fourth brother I keep talking about. It seems to me that modernity, understood as a specific era in Western history, is both an heir of biblical patrimony and a force for secularization. This has important implications for how we should understand the universality of divine strategy.

Modernity in the West has tended to assume its own universality, forgetting its particular biblical roots. *Modern* is still used, much of the time, as a term of approbation, designating the present toward which all progress is tending, freeing us from the narrowness of the past—liberating us from many different pasts, in fact, many different religions and traditional customs and rigid social structures, all of which will be dissolved and overcome in the achievement of one modernity which is the same for everyone. This rather complacent assumption of universality, along with a kind of active forgetfulness of the past, is on display in eighteenth-century Deism, which was quintessentially modern in presenting itself as the universal religion

---

1. Schaff, *Creeds of Christendom*, vol. 2, 210.

of reason—when surely anyone from the East (a Buddhist or Hindu, for example) could have seen quite clearly that it was not universal at all but an inherently Western phenomenon, a partly secularized form of Christianity, with its belief in one God, the immortality of the soul, and rewards for virtue in a life after death—all Christian notions, but shorn of Christian priests and ministers and worship and doctrine. So secular modernity is still residually Christian in many ways, because modernity itself is not as universal as it thinks, but rather is *Western Christendom in the process of secularizing itself.*

Nietzsche saw this, I think, when he followed up his announcement of the death of God by insisting that it was precisely Christians who killed him. It was the pious Christian scholars of the nineteenth century who made the biblical God unbelievable with their historical criticism of the Scriptures; for they were ascetics at heart, driven by an inward, repressive self-cruelty going so far as to deny themselves the supreme comfort of their own favorite lie, their belief in God. That is one way of describing the developments that began to make it difficult for educated people in Western Europe to take the Bible literally, and which made the atlas you mention quite out of date already on the day it was published, less than a decade after Darwin's *Origin of Species*. The abbé Michel had not heard the news that God is dead, that history is secular and its outlines could no longer be determined by a literal reading of the Bible. I think Nietzsche was right at least to this extent, that this secularization was brought about largely by Christian scholars. The abbé was practicing a kind of biblical literalism that was already out of date by Christian standards.

Yet if modernity is secular, what it secularizes is its own Christian past, and a kind of residual Christianity is still everywhere to be found in it, even among the forces of secularization. The very word *Utopia*, which so aptly designates some of the deepest hopes of secular modernity, was invented by a Catholic saint, Thomas More. Later, Deists such as Voltaire attacked the abuses of the church by appealing to principles of Christian morality like "love thy neighbor." This residue of Christian morality is still very much with us—God's shadow, Nietzsche called it,[2] hoping to dispel it along with God. You and I are in fact conducting our discussion still under this shadow, or I would prefer to say, on the ground of the biblical patrimony. And of course I am suggesting that biblical narratives, though no longer read with the literalism of the abbé Michel, are still the best way

2. Nietzsche, *Gay Science*, §108.

4 – Truth, Tolerance, and Utopia

to understand the direction of divine strategy. The biblical God is not so dead as Nietzsche hoped.

So modernity aspires to secular universality, but it still bears the residue of biblical particularity within itself, often a bit undigested. For much of modernity, most notably in the nineteenth century when the aspiration to universal history was especially intense, the crucial name for this undigested particularity was "the Jew." Concerns about "the Jewish question" became a way for modern thinkers to consider the unenlightened, the tribal, the narrow and opaque—the other who is recalcitrant in his otherness, not easily made universal. This is one reason I think the particular relation of Jew and Gentile remains at the operational center of the divine strategy in universal history as well as in the Bible. The particularities of biblical history do not extend into universal history in the literal way assumed by the abbé Michel, yet the West, for all its aspirations to universality—in many ways quite successful aspirations, as its science and technology spread throughout the world—has not simply left the biblical narrative behind, as long as it still has its Jewish problem.

I am hoping the West has its Jewish problem for a long time to come. The Jews I know are not so sure—not so confident in the expansion of Judaism as you seem to suggest. Like the growth of Islam in Europe, the growth in Judaism comes more from procreation than from proselytizing. But Jews are having a problem procreating, because so many of their children are marrying Gentiles, so that their grandchildren are no longer Jewish. It would be narrow and intolerant to oppose such marriages, would it not? And yet I hope Jews can find it in themselves to be intolerant in this way, because I think it would be good to have more Jews in the world. Christianity cannot do without these recalcitrant others.

That is the direction, I think, in which the divine strategy is taking us with regard to the Jew first, but then all recalcitrant others: the recognition that I cannot be without this difficult brother of mine, this other in all his otherness. In Jesus' parable, this recognition takes the form of gladness that this brother, who is God's son, is alive not dead. If I understand properly, God's strategy aims at the coming of a different kingdom than the Utopia where intolerance disappears along with priests and rituals. It is a kingdom where Jews will still be Jews (with all their Jewish rituals) and Gentiles will still be Gentiles, where the otherness of the other will remain even in his recalcitrance and "intolerance."

Does God Have a Strategy?

But let me now ask you a question. Early in our discussion we agreed—did we not?—that the great Eastern religions did not really have a place for a conception of divine strategy, a direction in which God was guiding human history as a whole. To that extent your proposal remains quite Western, bearing traces or residues of biblical eschatology and its hope of a final revelation. Aren't you too drawing on the biblical patrimony here? How do you propose to sustain this hope? I am wondering how it can be sustained without particular religious communities to keep it alive, without rituals and priests and mediators between God and humanity.

Jean-François Phelizon—Is it utopia or is it realism? I have the impression, at any rate, that God is necessarily greater than the universe he created.

Confining God to a small portion of the earth, even one that's full of history, doesn't work for me. Among the billions and billions of solar systems that make up the universe, there are millions and millions of planets resembling this earth we inhabit, each with its own history and living things, some of which are (not *have been* or *will be*) more fully evolved than we are. It would take fourteen billion years traveling at the speed of light to get to the farthest reaches of the universe. Such an immensity of space is not a utopia. Not for God, at any rate.

Restricting God to biblical history doesn't work for me. The world was not created 6,000 years ago. The human race with its extraordinary vanity will have disappeared after a very, very long time when the sun, having reached critical mass, will explode some time after having absorbed our planet. But the preprogrammed end *of our earth* will not, for all that, be the *end of the world*. Billions of other stars will in the meantime have taken the place of our sun, shining on countless other inhabited planets, whose existence we will never be able to suspect. Such an immensity of time is not a utopia. Not for God, at any rate.

To assimilate God to human concepts, venturing to simplify him when we scarcely have an inkling of the tiniest bit of the complexity all around us, doesn't work for me. We make claims to define the laws of the universe, to comprehend its evolution. We have certainly made enormous progress in mathematics, physics, chemistry, and biology, but we will never come to the end of our labors. Our science will never be enough to explain the world in which we live. And between the infinitely small and the infinitely large,

4 – Truth, Tolerance, and Utopia

we will never have a *definitive* idea of the way it all works in reality. Such an immensity of complexity is not a utopia. Not for God, at any rate.

So I have this huge idea of God, in fact, but what I can't imagine is God being less than infinitely great, less eternal than the infinity of time, or simpler than the infinite complexity all around us that we have scarcely begun to be aware of. I know that, for many theologians, particularly Thomas Aquinas, God is on the contrary infinitely simple. It seems to me hard to adopt this point of view, given the infinite complexity of the universe. If God were infinitely simple, how could he grasp or understand the infinitely complex?

For me, utopia means not believing that beyond this universe, which we have barely begun to catch sight of, there undoubtedly exists an all-powerful force that controls *everything*. Indeed, we look like the prisoners in Plato's cave (in an allegory presented in book 7 of the *Republic*), where people are chained up so that they can't see except in front of them. The light of a fire comes from above and behind them. It passes through an opening in the cave in such a way that the body of each prisoner casts a shadow on the wall. The chains symbolize beliefs, certitudes, convictions, prejudices, and other *a prioris*.

Utopia is perhaps to affirm that in the infinitude of space-time, God one day had the idea of choosing one nation in Judea and protecting it in all its troubles. Utopia is perhaps this nation believing it is the one and only chosen people of God, in disdain of all the surrounding nations which then existed on earth, known or unknown, and also all those more highly developed and worthy than themselves.

So: if God has a strategy, we must undoubtedly picture him—and this not through lack of realism—as watching over all the peoples of the earth, past, present, and future, and also over all the other inhabited worlds, the probable existence of which it would be highly presumptuous of us to deny nowadays. It is not impossible, as I understand it, for God himself to be a utopia. I would simply like to say that if the God that is greater than all infinities I just mentioned does not exist, then *a fortiori* the God of any one religion, whichever one it might be, does not exist either, for he would be infinitely smaller than the universe within which, as if by accident, we find ourselves living.

In the Eastern religions (I mean essentially Hinduism, Buddhism, Confucianism, Shintoism, and Taoism) God is not really defined with as much exactitude as in the Western religions. He does not manifest himself;

Does God Have a Strategy?

he is *absent*. These religions take note of the mystery of the universe and the limitations of human nature. They don't seek to resolve this mystery or to abolish human limitations. They propose rather to help human beings transcend themselves, to reach an ideal level—not a utopian one—where they feel themselves in harmony not just with themselves but with the world around them. This is why the Eastern religions bear more resemblance to philosophies that are basically Platonist than to religions as we understand them in the West.

To take some examples: *Hinduism* sees Brahman as nothing other than "the first cause of all being." Brahman is infinite and impersonal and encompasses all things, but it is associated with Vishnu, Shiva, and countless other gods that are not infinite. Likewise, for *Buddhism* there is no god, no creator, no creation, no "ego," no heaven or hell. The Buddhist aims to attain Nirvana after various reincarnations, which means arriving at the state of nothingness from which it is impossible to be reborn any more. The very notion of a supreme Being is inconsistent with the basic attributes of existence, which are impersonality and impermanence. As for *Confucianism,* it is primarily interested in human beings and their practical lives. Confucius based his teaching on ancient Chinese practices of veneration for heaven and ancestor worship. For him, "heaven" is a sort of impersonal power. According to *Taoism*, the gods govern and control everything in the universe. Among them, the god of the primordial beginning, the god of the sacred jade, and the god of the way of power mentioned by Lao Tzu are considered the supreme gods, but there is no supreme Being either. Finally, *Shintoism* is based on the deification of the forces of nature and ancestor worship. In large part it adopts the morality of Confucianism, Taoism, and Buddhism. Shintoists venerate countless personal gods, but none of them is infinite.

In none of these religions does a divine design appear. As a result, I cannot see how it could be said that a divine strategy manifests itself clearly through the religions practiced in the two immense cultural zones that are India and China. Yet how can we not take account of them?

If you believe in only one God, then you certainly ought to refer to the monotheist religions, i.e., essentially to the Abrahamic religions. But it is necessary eventually to get beyond them. In the end the problem of God is *whether he is infinite and thus probably infinitely distant from human beings and the religions they have instituted, or whether he is the God of a human religion* (of a single religion, I should say) *and then he cannot be infinite.*

4 – Truth, Tolerance, and Utopia

Phillip Cary—When I called your view utopian, I did not mean it was unrealistic. I was thinking of the etymology of the word *utopia*, which literally means "nowhere." What I had in mind was a universal idea not tied down to a particular location, to a unique holy place like Jerusalem or Mecca, a unique sacred language like Hebrew or Arabic, or a unique chosen people like Israel or the church. If you are willing to accept this usage, I would still use the word to describe your vision of the infinity of God and its implications. For you—or at least for God, as you understand him—not even the earth is a uniquely special place. In that sense yours is a utopian God, belonging nowhere in particular because he belongs everywhere equally.

Naturally there is a certain sense in which I agree with you. Of course God is present everywhere in the universe, at all points in space-time, omnipresent as well as eternal. "Do I not fill heaven and earth?" says the God of Israel to the prophet Jeremiah (Jer 23:24). Likewise when Solomon dedicates the temple he has built for the Lord in Jerusalem, he says, "Heaven and the highest heaven cannot contain you, how much less this house that I have built!" (1 Kgs 8:27). Yet he also prays "that your eyes may be open night and day toward this house, the place of which you have said, 'My name shall be there,' that you may listen to the prayer that your servant offers toward this place" (1 Kgs 8:29).

What I see in this prayer is an account of the omnipresence of God that is not utopian. The God of Israel lives everywhere, both filling all things and beyond all things, yet his attention is focused in a special way on the temple in Jerusalem—the house of the LORD, as it is called. Just as he has a particular name (the name written *YHWH* but pronounced *Adonai*, meaning "Lord," and traditionally written in English with four capital letters, LORD) as well as a particular people whom he has chosen to bind with himself in an eternal covenant, so also there is a particular place to find him, a temple in the holy city, where his people may come into his presence in worship, thanksgiving, and prayer. One image the Bible uses is that the throne of God is above the heavens but the temple is his footstool on earth (1 Chr 28:2; Pss 99:5, 132:7; Isa 60:13; and Ezek 43:7). The holy place in the midst of Jerusalem does not confine him, but it is closer to his presence in heaven than any other place on earth.

Christianity shares this picture, but in a peculiar way turns it on its head. For Christian faith the supreme holy place, the equivalent to the temple, is the body of Jesus Christ. And because he is now raised bodily from

Does God Have a Strategy?

the dead and has ascended into heaven, his living human flesh is "located" at the right hand of God, far above the heavens—which is to say, it is not found at any particular place in the cosmos. In that sense Christianity is more utopian than Judaism. Yet it is not fully utopian, for the holy place is still quite particular, the living flesh of a particular Jew, whose very being is the presence of God in the world.

None of the Abrahamic religions are fully utopian, in the sense I am using the word, because all of them are devoted to certain particularities in which they find God: particular holy places (a temple or city), particular holy persons (prophets, priests, saints, the Messiah), and particular rituals (bread and wine, circumcision and baptism, daily prayers). All of these particularities and their differences would be dissolved in the triumph of a utopianism that sees God everywhere and nowhere.

The Abrahamic religions in effect claim to have it both ways: a God who is both infinite (present in and beyond all things) and also found in a unique way in a few particular things, places, and people. This is a consequence of the metaphysical peculiarity that I pointed out a while ago, that the God of the Abrahamic religions is "both the source of all being and an agent within the story of the world." If God is to act in definite ways in the story of the world, he will have to be involved with particular people, at particular places and times. You can't be part of a story without being involved in such particularities. This involvement is essential to what Judaism and Christianity mean by "love," which is not an impartial justice towards all but a wholehearted and unqualified choice of one from among the many: of one particular people as uniquely beloved, elect, partners in his covenant—his bride, the apple of his eye (see Deut 32:10 and Zech 2:8), whom he can never leave or forsake for all eternity. And my contention about the divine strategy is that this choice of God to love one particular people is good news for all others. Divine love comes to us all precisely through one particular people chosen and most beloved, the Jews.

Therefore, just as in a non-utopian view, not all places are alike to God, so also not all people are equal. As I put it earlier, the human race is divided not into the saved and the damned, but into Israel and all others. The question you are asking me at this point, I take it, is about all those others, including not only the adherents of the great Eastern religions but also the others we do not yet know, perhaps may never know, but who are (as you suggest) surely out there among the millions of planets in the millions of galaxies where intelligent life is possible. What kind of strategy can the

4 – Truth, Tolerance, and Utopia

God of Israel, with his absurd devotion to a particular beloved nation on this earth, have for such people?

What answer I can give you comes from my place as one among those others. I am not a Jew, which means I may hope for the blessing and grace of God only as all those others do, as something that spreads outward, as it were, from Jerusalem to touch all other places and their peoples, including the hypothetical ones in distant galaxies we will never know. In some way, I am confident, they also are blessed through Israel and Israel's Messiah, who are chosen for the blessing of all nations. How this might work out in particular, of course, I cannot say: that is part of a story that is quite unavailable to us, a story that may one day include more than the human race, if we ever encounter such people in an unimaginably distant future. But here I must leave the details of divine strategy to God!

But to come back to earth: about the great Eastern religions we know some of the story. Since the global encounter of East and West in the past few centuries, their history has been influenced by the Christianity of the West and its role in both missionary activity and colonial administration. Nowadays the colonial administrators are gone, along with most of the missionaries, but the presence of Christianity, along with Western culture, science and technology, has become a lasting part of the life of most Asian countries. China and South Korea in particular have large, flourishing churches of their own, along with universities, industries, and technologies of their own. Many of these Asian churches are as independent of the West as Asian industry is, and perhaps more so. They have native-born pastors and operate quite without supervision from abroad. And in China especially, the churches are proliferating at a rate that alarms the government. It looks to many observers as if the religious future of China might be more Christian than Buddhist. Here then are many millions of Gentiles, more "others" who find blessing and divine love in the Messiah of the Jews. Who can say what will come of this in the end? I will not venture predictions. But I may surely hope that the divine strategy that was a blessing for other Gentiles will be a blessing for these Gentiles as well.

What I can say a bit more about is the metaphysics of Eastern religions, which do not share the peculiar notion that the source of all being is also an agent within the story of the world. As you point out, they tend to make a sharp distinction between an impersonal supreme principle (Brahman in Hinduism, "heaven" in Confucianism, etc.) and the gods or ancestors or avatars who are objects of particular devotion, participants with human

Does God Have a Strategy?

beings in the history of the world. For the Eastern religions only such gods, who are not infinite and supreme, could conceivably have a strategy, and their strategy cannot be what gives ultimate form to the world.

Here again the Abrahamic religions insist on having it both ways, teaching that the supreme principle, the source of all being, is not merely some*thing* but some*one*, a person with a strategy who encounters us as other than himself (which cannot happen with Brahman, for example) and who can therefore contend with us human beings, can love and punish and forgive and persuade and redeem—so that love, justice, forgiveness, and redemption can be the story of the whole world.

Christianity in particular comes to the East proclaiming this good news: that the blessing you might hope for from propitious gods or ancestors can come to you from the supreme source of being, the creator of all that is, which is vastly greater than anything in the world. Or to put it the other way round: the supreme, infinite, transcendent principle that is above all things and beyond all things and other than all things has come to us as the kind of other who has a particular place in the world, one to whom we can offer love and devotion, one whom we can hear, and to whom we can speak, one for whom we can long like a bride awaiting the coming of her bridegroom. And all are invited to the wedding supper.

5
Paradigms of God

Jean-François Phelizon—Since at this point in our discussion it appears that we have different views of God, we cannot but have different conceptions of divine strategy as well.

As for me, my tendency is to think of God as an infinite being. To be infinite means to be disconnected in a certain way from our present time, or more precisely from our time and space. I am actually located in a double tradition that thinks we human beings *are nothing* (recall Pascal: "the eternal silence of these infinite spaces fills me with dread"[1]) and furthermore are the product of an evolution that reaches absolutely beyond us: we did not exist a hundred thousand years ago and will not exist in another hundred thousand years—a hundred thousand years: no more than the blink of an eye on the time scale of the universe!

In fact, it seems to me very presumptuous to believe that humanity is a finished product. Were we to live a few dozen more millennia, we would have profoundly changed in biological terms (always supposing, of course, that we have not disappeared from the face of the earth). Our religions have forgotten that there is life elsewhere than here where humanity has evolved, that there will be life after humanity, and that the existence of human beings will be (or has been) infinitely small in comparison with the duration of the life of the universe. Our religions have also forgotten that human beings are constantly evolving, like all living things. If we believe Pierre Teilhard de Chardin, then the evolution which makes it possible for one consciousness

1. Pascal, *Pensées*, §201.

Does God Have a Strategy?

to communicate with another creates *ipso facto* a kind of super-being: by grouping together through communication, consciousnesses are going to make the same qualitative leap as the molecules that, linking up together, suddenly changed from inert to living beings.

Humanity is not a finished product: that is the reason why I said that our problem with regard to God is whether he is infinite and thus probably infinitely distant from human beings and the religions that they have instituted to worship him, or whether he is the God of one human religion, in which case he cannot be infinite. It seems to me that the God of Israel, of the Gospels, or of the Qur'an must have existed long before Israel, long before Abraham, long before Adam and Eve, and he will continue to exist long after the disappearance of the human race and thus long after the end of all religions. Thus I cannot agree to *reduce* God to the dimension of history because I think I discern in this reduction a very inauspicious, anthropic idiosyncrasy.

Yet the anthropic aspect of God in the Abrahamic religions is quite present in the "sacred" texts on which they are founded. To take but one example: David says to Goliath the Philistine, before striking him down with a shot from his sling, "You came to me with a sword and with a spear and with a javelin, but I come to you in the name of the LORD of hosts, the God of the armies of Israel, whom you have defied. This day the LORD will deliver you into my hand, and I will strike you down and cut off your head. And I will give the dead bodies of the host of the Philistines this day to the birds of the air and to the wild beasts of the earth, that all the earth may know that there is a God in Israel" (1 Sam 17:45–46). I have no doubt that David existed, nor that he took up the challenge of the Philistines by fighting Goliath in a duel rather like the *trial by combat* of the Middle Ages, nor even that he triumphed *because he had faith*. But in the fact that God "will deliver" Goliath to David, and above all that God *takes sides* with Israel (and against the Philistines) I see a sad indication that this God is not infinite, that he perhaps accompanies a people over the course of their history but that in doing so he enters a context of human creation; he is only a reduction (a "scale model") of the infinite God, as I conceive him. It is a little as if one were to judge a person based on a vignette of his daily life, leaving out of the picture the great things he accomplished elsewhere—as if, for example, one reduced the character of Napoleon to nothing but the encouragement he lavished on the soldiers of his Old Guard by pinching them on the ear before they went into battle.

5 – Paradigms of God

Moreover, I think that to contrast believers with pagans (or Israel with "Gentiles") because they don't have the same conception of God, is quite simply to deprive God of his attribute of uniqueness. It is, by ascribing to him a human image, to *secularize* him.

Ancient Greece, in the *Iliad*, provides a fine example of gods taking sides and taking their turn in human battles. Ares, the son of Zeus, a fighter and warrior, was not very popular in Greece but much honored in Rome (being the father of Romulus and the Roman people). As the god of war, fierce and impetuous, he was the scourge of men, symbolizing violent death. Hermes, who was also the son of Zeus, was the god of human social relationships, of trade and commerce, of profit (which itself is the product of work, of risk and of deception). He was also the god of speech and eloquence, and in that capacity was the inventor of language. What defined Hermes was his prudence and resourcefulness. What defined Ares was his fiery spirit and lack of subtlety. In the *Iliad* Ares supports the Trojans with Aphrodite, while Athena and Hermes support the Greeks. The battle of Athena and Hermes against Ares and Aphrodite is the victorious struggle *of wisdom against irrationality.*

In the same way, the God for which David is the champion struggles victoriously against the God of the Philistines, whose champion is Goliath (the Bible does not explicitly mention the God of the Philistines here, but hints that he is a scourge, like Ares: the scourge of Israel, of course). Thus when God takes sides in human history, he loses his character of uniqueness and becomes ambivalent. Being on one side rather than the other, God *a fortiori* cannot be limitless and infinite in time or in space.

What bothers me about your perspective on God is precisely that it gives me the impression of a limited being. When you write, *"the human race is divided not into the saved and the damned, but into Israel and all others,"* I find this ambivalence flowing from a God who takes sides: if God is only the God of Israel, then he cannot be one who transcends humanity. More broadly, the Abrahamic religions teach that God is everything and its opposite: now near, now far; now good, now cruel, etc. This permanent (and recurrent) ambivalence has served the earthly power of these religions and has even justified their worst excesses. It doesn't clarify anything for the believer, who just has to accept the *mystery* of God's existence no matter what.

Likewise when you write, *"this choice of God to love one particular people is good news for all others. Divine love comes to us all precisely through one particular people chosen and most beloved, the Jews,"* I equate this choice

Does God Have a Strategy?

of God for Israel (a choice that is quite in line with David's thinking as he faces Goliath) with favoritism in the strict sense of the term.

Again, I am not denying that God has made Israel his favored people; I am merely saying that in that case, if it is the God of Israel that you're talking about, it is not the God of all humanity, still less of the whole universe. For the consequence of this "choice" of God for Israel is that *ipso facto* it causes him to lose his attribute of uniqueness. To choose one tribe, to show partiality, to display an ambivalence, is to affirm a dependence. It is impossible to be above the human race and not be independent of it. It is impossible to take sides and still be unique. It is impossible to be infinitely good and *choose* a set of believers from among people of one faction. I cannot imagine that God would choose certain people (and thus be *committed* to them) as a function of their belonging to a group, a race, or a religion. I think rather that he should want to distinguish them independently of their belonging—as a function of their virtue, their integrity, or their wisdom.

These two contrasting conceptions of God (wholly infinite and thus distant on the one hand, committed and ambivalent on the other) clearly have important consequences for the strategy that can be attributed to God:

1. The strategy of the God of Israel is clear enough: you have yourself defined it as the ultimate reconciliation of Israel and the "Gentiles." (The strategy of the God of Islam, on the other hand, is still in question).

2. The strategy of the one *unique* God of the three Abrahamic religions is much less clear. For if we accept that the faithful of these three religions actually do worship the same God, then how can God take sides among the fratricidal, agonistic factions that keep fighting each other over the course of the centuries? But one could still accept that the long-term strategy is to reconcile these jealous brothers: Jews, Christians, and Muslims.

3. The strategy of the one unique God for all humanity is frankly problematic. Is it the survival of the species? Its moral uplift? Its "salvation" (but then what exactly does this word mean)? If the God we believe in is in fact infinite in time and space, it really is quite difficult to attribute a strategy to him, since we others, human beings, are so insignificant with respect to him.

Since strategy is first of all a direction, we can see that the nearer God is (the *smaller* he is, I'm tempted to write), the more he takes sides, and the clearer his strategy is for those who believe in him, such as David; but the more God is infinite and therefore distant (the *greater* he is) the less a

5 – Paradigms of God

strategy can be attributed to him that is comprehensible to the human race. This should not be a surprise: since strategy is in essence a human notion, only a God in the image of human beings can, like a commander in chief, *lead* human beings in a given direction. Conversely, the God who created the universe some fourteen billion years ago, a universe that probably includes millions of inhabited worlds, cannot even think of "choosing" the human race, still less of assigning it a guideline. He is incommensurable with us, not on the same scale. No doubt we can imagine he exists, but we are incapable of comprehending whether he is following a direction and still less of glimpsing the direction that he takes (supposing that he has one).

Phillip Cary—It is indeed an important question, a metaphysical question that can be asked in many different ways: is God "big" or "little"? Is God infinite, beyond all particular places and times and peoples, or does God have a special concern for a particular chosen people, with their particular history and their particular holy place? Is God universal, the same for everyone, or does God play favorites and take sides—fighting, say, on behalf of David and Israel against Goliath and the Philistines?

I said earlier that the Abrahamic religions want "to have it both ways." So perhaps it will not surprise you when I answer that God is *both* big *and* little. As we say in English, this is a both/and, not an either/or. But I will admit that on the face of it, "either/or" seems to be a very natural way to put the question.

"Either/or" expresses the sense that you can't have it both ways: surely *either* God is infinite *or* he belongs in one particular place with one particular people—not both. That is the same as to say: surely the infinite God *cannot* belong to one particular place or one particular people. For how could the universal source of all things be so limited and confined? (That is the key metaphysical question.) And how could the one God, who is the same for all, play favorites—taking sides with one warring nation against others? (That is the ethical implication of the metaphysical question.)

"Either/or" is a natural way to put the question because the Abrahamic religions do indeed reject the notion that the true God could ever be one of the "little" gods of polytheism, like Ares fighting on the side of Hector and the Trojans, or Athena stepping up beside Diomedes on his chariot. Such gods end up fighting against each other, as we see in the fifth book of the *Iliad*. No doubt anyone who reads the book we are writing together is, like

Does God Have a Strategy?

us, enough a child of Abraham to find such a thing impossible. The little gods cannot truly be God at all. At best they may represent aspects of the world around us or of human character, such as the impetuous belligerence of Ares or the subtle wisdom of Athena. This is how Greek philosophers (especially the Stoics and Platonists) interpreted the Homeric gods, as a kind of allegory representing abstract principles. For they too saw an "either/or" here, and insisted that the little gods could not be that which is most truly divine, infinite, unique, transcendent, incomparably "big."

Here we come again upon the alliance between the Abrahamic religions and the Western philosophical tradition, which I mentioned near the beginning of our discussion. They agree that God is metaphysically "big," infinite, and unique, for he is the sole source of all that is, existing prior to and apart from and beyond the whole universe that comes from him, embracing it all in his knowledge and power but dependent on none of it for his being and life, utterly unlimited by space and time and therefore entirely present at all times and places, whole and undivided, one and unchanged. This metaphysical conception of God, worked out most elaborately in the Neoplatonist tradition stemming from Plotinus, has found its way into Jewish, Muslim, and Christian thinking by various means. It suits the conviction of these religions that God has no beginning (all three religions reject myths of the origin or birth of the gods such as one finds in Hesiod), that he is the creator of all things (in Neoplatonist terms, the first principle or source of all being and goodness), that he is invisible, not to be represented by any image (hence in Neoplatonist terms, incorporeal, without a material body and its limitations).

But the Abrahamic religions always add that God has chosen or elected to favor a particular people and place: the Jews and Jerusalem and its temple, the Arabs and Mecca and the Ka'aba, the Christians and the body of Christ that is the fundamental "place" of his presence to the world. The children of Abraham can sound very much like believers in the "little" gods when they talk about how God guides them, takes their side, even fights their battles—and there is certainly plenty of such talk in the Bible and the Qur'an. So this is the both/and. They are believers in a God who is both big and little, the creator of all who nonetheless takes sides with one against others. I take this to be a daring metaphysical proposal, which distinguishes the Abrahamic religions from all other views of the divine. But it is fair to ask how the theologians of the Abrahamic religions think they can get away with saying this kind of thing.

5 – Paradigms of God

Let me present the orthodox Christian answer, which is the most daring of all, but which I believe is necessary for justifying the portrayal of God in the Old Testament. If God can be *both* the infinite first principle of all things *and* a person who has a beloved whom he chooses as his own, it is because of what we see in Jesus Christ. In short, the doctrine of the incarnation is Christianity's fundamental "both/and."

The most familiar version of this "both/and" was formulated by the Council of Chalcedon in 451, which taught that Christ is true God and true man, having both a fully divine nature and a fully human nature. An earlier formulation by the church father Gregory of Naziansen is also very helpful. Speaking of the eternal Logos or Word of God, the second person of the Trinity, Gregory says: "He remained what he was; he took up what he was not." He remains God, the eternal Son and Word of God who (according to the doctrine of the Trinity) is himself God, which is to say he is eternal, omnipresent, beyond space and time, infinite and unchangeable, impassible and immortal. Yet in Christ he takes up or assumes what he is not: human nature, which is not eternal but had a beginning and a birth, not omnipresent but located in a particular place, not unchangeable but subject to growth, aging, vulnerability, and death.

This is why Christianity, alone of the Abrahamic religions, can speak of the death of God. The immortal one dies; for, remaining what he was (the immortal God) he assumes what he was not (human mortality)—so that for three days the eternal Son of God, remaining immortal, was none other than a particular dead man, whose corpse was in a tomb and whose soul was with the dead (hence the creed says: "he descended into hell," that is to say, to the place of the dead). The same logic underlies the confession that Mary is "mother of God" (or *theotokos* in Greek, a key term in the Council of Ephesus in 431). For the baby she bore in her womb is none other than the eternal Son of God, who is God. She does not originate his divine nature, of course, but his human nature. As the Council of Chalcedon says, he "takes flesh from the virgin." From her, he assumes what he was not, while remaining what he always is—the immutable Word of God, eternally one with God the Father.

There is of course much more to say about this doctrine of incarnation, including especially its dependence on the orthodox doctrine of the Trinity. But for now let me simply point out some of its consequences, which are relevant to your question. It means that God is both big and little, both the universal first principle of all things (as any Neoplatonist might

Does God Have a Strategy?

put it) and a man dying on a cross. But it does not endorse the polytheist notion of little gods, because the littleness of God is not in his deity but in his humanity, the human flesh he assumes. The divine nature of Christ remains infinite, unconfined by space and time and therefore both eternal and omnipresent. God always remains "big," and becomes little only by assuming *our* littleness. He makes it his own (he assumes what he is not), but it does not confine or change him (he remains what he is).

This means also that the incarnation does not simply manifest an aspect or portion of God, a slice of his life like Napoleon's intimate actions in the hour before battle. According to the orthodox doctrine of incarnation, the man Jesus Christ quite simply *is* the eternal Son of God, one and the same person, even though his divine nature remains infinitely more than his human nature. In this one man the eternal God, remaining beyond all space and time, assumes a place within his creation and its history, living at a particular place and time, sharing in its particular passions, desires, hopes, and suffering. He becomes a particular Jew, one of the people he has chosen for himself. Indeed, he becomes *the* chosen one (see Luke 9:35), the beloved Son who fulfills in his own person the purpose for which God has chosen Israel.

This is how it is possible for God to have a chosen people: he becomes one of them. It is how he plays favorites—for he does indeed have a favorite son, Jesus Christ, through whom he blesses all others. But it is a very strange kind of favoritism, which involves immense suffering and often looks like defeat. It was not so unreasonable for the rulers of his own people to look at him on the cross and say, "He saved others; let him save himself, if he is the Christ of God, his Chosen One!" (Luke 23:35)

And it is only because of this, I would add, that God can have a strategy. To implement a strategy one must have a particular location in time and space, and involvement with particular people. We have agreed that it involves taking a *direction*, and it seems to me the concept of a direction requires some kind of starting place and a goal or end. And we have agreed that strategy is implemented on behalf of a community or group, operating in a world that includes other groups that may oppose it. Both of these, the direction and the group, require a location *within* the world and its history. The infinite first principle of Neoplatonist metaphysics, like the Brahman of Hindu metaphysics, does not have such a location and therefore cannot have a strategy. This is an impossibility, but not a failing or a defect; for strategy, like the particular loyalties strategy always serves, is *beneath* it.

5 – Paradigms of God

To use Plato's metaphor from the allegory of the cave, the first principle is like the sun shining equally on all things, bringing goodness and beauty, even order and justice, to the world below, but certainly not taking sides or favoring one group over others. If there is a difference between one thing and another, if one thing is better than another, it is because it is closer to the Good (Plato's name for the first principle), the way higher things are closer to the sun. The difference between the one and the other does not come from the Good or the One itself (to add the Neoplatonist term for the first principle), for this One is not a particular one among others. Therefore it takes no sides and has no favorites, as it remains immutably the same for all. It is not a person and has no beloved to fight for. It is universally beneficent, but beyond every particular love and loyalty, and therefore has no need to descend to the level of strategy.

The Abrahamic religions say otherwise—most emphatically in the Christian doctrine of incarnation, according to which the first principle becomes one of the many things he has made, entering the history of the world as one of the actors on its stage. Therefore he can take sides, make choices, and be a particular person with particular loves and loyalties, including a particular beloved for whom he fights. And that requires a strategy.

It also raises the ethical question that I mentioned above, a question that has never been far from my discussion of divine strategy. To say that God has a favorite son or a chosen people, so that he is rightly called the God *of Israel*, sounds at first as if he were just like the "little" national gods of the surrounding peoples of the ancient middle East, such as Dagon of the Philistines or Chemosh of the Moabites or Baal of the Canaanites. His strategy then would be to protect his people and expand their power at the expense of others. His aim would be to defeat the enemies of his favorites. Such a god is a threat to the rest of humanity.

But such is not the God of Israel, who chooses his beloved people so that they may be a blessing for all nations. Such is not the God and Father of our Lord Jesus Christ, who suffers and dies for the salvation of the whole world. Israel, like Christ, has a history of suffering as well as triumph, for both are indispensable to the divine strategy. The God of Israel does not simply fight for his favorite people but shapes them into the blessing that he intends in the end for all people, and that requires the experience of suffering, defeat, mourning, and loss.

So we can discern an overall direction of divine strategy, I think, though it reaches further than we can see. The direction takes its starting point from the stories of jealous brothers in Genesis (Cain and Abel, Jacob and Esau, Joseph and his brothers) and issues in the nation of Israel, the children of Abraham, Isaac, and Jacob who are to be a blessing for all nations, and it culminates in Christ, the son of Israel who triumphs only by suffering for all. How exactly God takes that direction beyond the scriptural story is less clear (Christians argue with one another about it all the time) but it surely has something to do also with that third jealous brother we have been talking about, the people of Islam. Not only that, but the divine strategy clearly includes a blessing for all humanity, including those who do not lay claim to the patrimony of Abraham, such as Buddhists and Hindus. And finally, if there are other intelligent creatures living on planets light years away from us, the divine strategy no doubt includes them. I do not suppose we can say how it includes them, because I do not know who they are or whether their existence is more than hypothetical. But I am confident that the divine strategy will, whatever form it takes, have the same fundamental direction, to which it will be right to give the name, love.

Jean-François Phelizon—I think we've come to an essential point in our conversation—I would even say the turning point of our discussion.

I quite agree that *according to the points of view* that are adopted, God can be considered "big" (let us say we are then in the presence of the *first paradigm*) or "little" (which is the *second paradigm*). I will assume that this all concerns the same God, as you suggest. It seems to me then that a certain number of consequences flow from this.

Consider first the immensity of God. According to the first paradigm, God is eternal and infinite. He completely transcends us, beyond all that we can imagine. I tried to apprise my daughter of what I call *the three infinities* of space, time, and complexity. The idea really bothered her. The other day she asked me which was bigger, the sun or the moon. I explained that it was the sun, that it was (almost) infinitely bigger than the moon. Then she asked me if the world was bigger than the sun. I answered that the universe is (almost) infinitely bigger than the sun. Now, as an infinite "being," God is infinitely "bigger" (and also infinitely more complex) than the world he has created: we cannot conceive of him, which means when we try to comprehend him at our level, he can only be an idea, a concept. The truth is that we can hardly imagine his existence.

According to the second paradigm, God is of quite a different size. He is by contrast close to us, as you have put it so well. We can pray to him,

5 – Paradigms of God

which means "talking" with him, or at any rate making an appeal to him. In the *Dogmatic Constitution on Divine Revelation (Dei Verbum)*, an official document of the Catholic Church published as a result of the Vatican II council, we read: "It pleased God, in his goodness and wisdom, to reveal himself.... By this revelation, then, the invisible God, from the fullness of his love addresses men as his friends and moves among them in order to invite and receive them into his own company."[2] Here we are on familiar ground. If I may put it this way, we have a God that is within reach. Hence Charles de Foucauld can claim: "You are there, my Lord Jesus, one meter away from me in this tabernacle [containing the Eucharistic host]."[3] Furthermore, God takes sides: he fights on David's side against Goliath. He supports Israel against the Philistines. In fact there is little difference in essence between the gods who helped the Greeks defeat the Trojans and Yahweh who lends a hand to David so he can defeat Goliath.

In the one case, the partisanship of the gods symbolizes, as I said, the victorious struggle of the wisdom of the Greeks against the irrationality of the barbarians; in the other, the partisanship of Yahweh symbolizes the rightness of a war that opposes the virtue of the elect to the barbarity of the idolaters. A powerful being, indeed all-powerful ("Nothing is impossible with God," according to the *Catechism of the Catholic Church*[4]), a transcendent being so far beyond humans, who nonetheless seems to be interested in them and their quarrels, *chooses* to put himself on one side rather than another, *decides* to support one faction rather than another, in one or another of the essentially miserable struggles that have ravaged the human race from the depths of time. As you put it, the Abrahamic religions always claim that God "has chosen or elected to favor a particular people." If this transcendent being takes up the cause of one faction, it is because he appreciates the submission of its members, their behavior, their previous actions. If he takes sides, it is because he prefers those who call themselves his allies and decides to support them against those "others" who *ipso facto* become his enemies.

I would like to insist once again on the immense difference there is between the God of the first paradigm, who is infinite and distant (so distant that one can legitimately ask why he would bother with the human race) and the God of the second paradigm (so close to us that it looks easy for

---

2. Flannery, ed., *Vatican II*, 750-1.
3. Translated from Foucauld, *Écrits spirituels*, 69.
4. *Catechism of the Catholic Church*, §269.

us to *move* him to act in our favor: "Lord have mercy!" as Christians say). The difference is so great that one may doubt whether this really is the same "being" or the same concept. In relation to the first paradigm, we human beings are infinitely small (we don't even know for sure that God notices us, so great is our insignificance in relation to him). In relation to the second paradigm, by contrast, we acknowledge that God is more powerful than we are, but we think that in virtue of the will and might of this all-powerful being we can get him to change the course of events and act on our behalf: we think that he can favor us, that he can serve our interests.

Thus, if we believe in God—or to put it plainly, if we understand that he can act for us if we submit ourselves to what we believe is his will—then we can put his omnipotence at our service. The "terms of exchange" are then as follows: on the one hand we have faith and worship God; on the other hand he assures us of his benevolent protection and *saves* us. As the *Catechism* states, "faith is a gift of God, a supernatural virtue."[5] This faith is "necessary for obtaining ... salvation."[6]

The "priests" (of course I'm thinking of all priests, those in the ancient world as well as the Catholic Church) are intermediaries between the "little" God and ordinary human beings, the believers. Since they know how to "talk" to him, their function (if not their mission) consists not only in bringing us to him, but also in making intercession before him on our behalf. So if we submit to God, if we heed the priests who know how to interpret his will, then there's a chance our prayers will be heard and answered. We are even permitted to make a contract with the God of the second paradigm, whose sovereignty we acknowledge: "We exacted a covenant with the prophets and with thee (O Muhammad)" (Qur'an 33:7).

It goes without saying that nothing like this could happen in the context of the first paradigm. There are no priests there, no mediators or intercessors. We are so tiny, so ridiculously small! How could we influence God? As I said: one can hardly believe that in the space-time that is ours, a God who was eternal and infinitely powerful would be interested, even at a great distance, in beings as presumptuous, scheming, contentious, and arrogant as ourselves. Can you imagine a peasant from the Nile making an appeal to Pharaoh? A poor cleric successfully petitioning the bishop of Rome? A Chinese beggar from the seventeenth century getting the emperor to take an interest in his misery? Of course not. And yet the distance that separates

5. Ibid., §153.
6. Ibid., §161.

5 – Paradigms of God

the peasant of the Nile from Pharaoh, the poor cleric from the pope, and the beggar from the emperor is infinitely less than that which separates us from God in the context of the first paradigm.

Thus the God of the first paradigm is inevitably distant (he is extraordinarily distant); while the God of the second paradigm is by nature near to us (he is astonishingly near). This nearness is the reason why God comes to *exist* for us. If humanity from its origins had not elaborated an *approachable* expression of God and the next world, God would have remained nothing but the "concept" I mentioned. Fortunately, thanks especially to the intercessors who are the priests of the world (and I should add the prophets of all religions) we other human beings have the privilege of being able to appeal to God on a regular basis, to feel him within reach of our prayers, to believe that he watches over us, that he protects us and even, at the most basic level, that he takes an interest in us personally.

Let me go back now to Plato's allegory of the cave. The God of the first paradigm (the "true" God in all his greatness) is the one who, like the sun, shines equally on all things, affording beauty, harmony, and the order of the universe to the human race—not in our daily life, not to make our lives easier or to win our battles, but on a conceptual level. Plato explains:

> The visible realm should be likened to the prison dwelling, and the light of the fire inside it to the power of the sun. And if you interpret the upward journey and the study of things above as the upward journey of the soul to the intelligible realm, you'll grasp what I hope to convey. . . . In the knowable realm, the form of the Good is the last thing to be seen, and it is reached only with difficulty. Once one has seen it, however, one must conclude that it is the universal cause of all that is correct and beautiful in anything, that it produces both light and its source in the visible realm, and that in the intelligible realm it provides truth and understanding, so that anyone who is to act wisely in private or public must see it.[7]

It would be instructive to reread this passage, replacing "the idea of the Good" with "God" (which a Neoplatonist such as the emperor Julian would surely have considered permissible).

The God of the second paradigm, although he surpasses us in power, is still aware of our requests, seeks to favor the men and women who believe in him, and can even help his deserving followers on a practical level. To be sure, the God of the first paradigm is big, the God of the second paradigm

---

7. Plato, *Republic*, in *Complete Works*, 7:517b-c.

Does God Have a Strategy?

is little, but as you point out, these are paradoxically two sides of the same being, two expression of the same reality. In principle, it must come down to the same God.

But what does *the same God* mean? Quite simply that the God of the second paradigm is only a representation, a reduction, a "projection" (in the geometrical sense of the term) of the God of the first paradigm—an image of him, just as the shadows dancing on the walls of Plato's cave, are images of the reality outside it. We can hardly imagine the "true" God; we can only envision a representation of him. This is why we can fully identify the God of the Jews (who is the champion of the Jews), the God of the Christians (who is the champion of the Christians), and the God of the Muslims (who is the champion of the Muslims). Clearly we are thinking of three different "Gods," and we are ready to fight to satisfy our champion (i.e., the God we believe in), even give our life for him—and we are also ready, if necessary, to kill all those who believe in a different God from ours. But once again, these are projections (three projections, if I consider the Abrahamic religions) or, if you will, *images* of the same God, that of the first paradigm.

So then, in my view the God of the second paradigm is one representation among others, a particular and specifically human *revelation* of the infinite God of the first paradigm. The God of the first paradigm, as an "idea," a "concept," is unique and transcendent; we can try to apprehend his existence using our reason (Aristotle thought he was the necessary First Cause of all things). Whereas the "Gods" of the second paradigm, as images of God projected in and by a given monotheist religion, are multifarious and ambivalent; they are "revealed" to the human race and without these "revelations" human beings could not have the knowledge needed for their salvation.

Of course there is an infinity of possible projections or imaginable revelations of God, and thus an infinity of potential religions furnishing images of God that are necessarily quite reduced—it would be preferable to say "infinitely reduced." That is why the God of the second paradigm is less universal and above all *less universally believable* than the God of the first paradigm.

The consequence of this phenomenon of projection is that the God of a religion, being by definition accessible, *ought* to assume a markedly anthropomorphic character. This is why we may legitimately doubt his veracity and universality. By contrast, the God of the first paradigm is so far beyond us that we couldn't *not* believe in him unless we thought that

5 – Paradigms of God

nothing could surpass the human race. As we are infinitely small in the midst of the universe, as the forces that rule over it are utterly beyond our understanding, it would be strikingly presumptuous to deny them. So it would be just as presumptuous not to accept that God exists.

So there is an *other world*, which we believe to be spiritual but which we cannot grasp, and *this world*, the temporal world in the cave where we are born, live, and die. Every endeavor to describe the *other world* is merely a poor attempt at extrapolating from *this world*. How can we imagine a three-dimensional volume on the basis of a two-dimensional surface—a sphere on the basis of a circle? And what can we say about this object, in a space of n dimensions, of which the projection in our world is a sphere?

The dichotomy between the "big" God and the "little" God leads us to *relativize* the images of God that are projected by different religions. Thus the God of the Jews becomes not identical but *analogous* to the God of the Christians or that of the Muslims. Why do these three images of the "little" God have the same validity? Why do they literally have the same weight? *Because this is about projections, revelations, separate but equivalent representations of the same God,* a little like the colors of the rainbow that represent the same source of light. Of course this equivalence of the images of God ends up making the Abrahamic religions themselves strikingly equivalent; it validates them all *a priori* in much the same way. It tends also to make the messages these religions deliver to their followers much the same, if not equivalent (messages of peace, of morality, and of intolerance as well).

From this standpoint, the question once again is knowing what could be the strategy of God. If we remain in the context of the first paradigm, I say again that the strategy of God is always incomprehensible to us. How could we even imagine the strategy (i.e., the will) of a being who is infinitely beyond us and who moreover is everywhere in time and space? To believe that we could comprehend even the tiniest bit of the will of God would be sheer vanity on our part. Nothing authorizes to think that we could decode or express this strategy, if it even so much as exists. Everything on the contrary leads us to think that it will remain forever a mystery to us.

On the other hand, if the viewpoint we adopt is that of the second paradigm, then the image of God that we bear in ourselves as believers—and which our priests fortunately help us to understand—would seem to us to correspond quite well with a direction and to express a will, a will that can show us favor, however little we may have faith in it. In this sense the strategy of God seen by a Christian seems perfectly understandable, just

Does God Have a Strategy?

like the strategy of God for a Jew or for a Muslim. Besides, the strategies are different: the God of the Christians does not have the same "objectives" in view nor even perhaps the same overall guideline as the God of the Jews or the Muslims. Since in addition the God of the second paradigm is a reduction *ad infinitum* of the God of the first paradigm, nothing allows us to affirm that the finite strategy of the God in which we believe is compatible or consistent with the strategy of God insofar as he is infinitely greater and infinitely more complex that the universe.

It is this *reduction* of God to a given religion that leads us to relativize his image in the context of the second paradigm. If in his eternity and timelessness God can be projected in many ways, there is no reason for one religion to be "more true" than the others or triumph over them. Each religion claims of course that it surpasses the others, that it possesses *the* truth, even if none seems to have legitimacy or arguments sufficient to justify this assertion.

This explains why for the Jews, the God of David is *the* protector, while for the Philistines, the God of Goliath is *the* protector. Likewise, thinking for a moment of the Crusades, the God of the Arabs is no more legitimate than that of the Europeans. Each of them is just a different projection of the same infinite God, that of the first paradigm. The people in Plato's cave "suppose that the names they used applied to the things they see passing before them," with the result that they "believe that the truth is nothing other than the shadows."[8]

Can a "big" God also be "little"? Yes, of course—just as the geometrical projection of a solid can be made at various levels and thus furnish various images of the same reality, all of which are true but all of which are partial and *limited* (and thus all of which are deformed as well). In short, human beings shut up together in the cave discover that there are many shadows, many openings to the world outside, many realities. One of these realities is Christian, another is Jewish, and a third is Muslim (and there are still others). Depending on which religion they belong to, they perceive different shadows of God. The shadows fool them because it's impossible for them to leave the cave. Yet in reality all of them are shadows of one and the same God, which they can never perceive and never comprehend because unfortunately they can never leave the cave. Each of their religions affirm that one of these shadows is the only image of God, the "true" one. It affirms also that all the other images are "false," which they are quite willing to believe. However, they never move out of the cave, they are shackled by

8. Ibid., 7:515b.

5 – Paradigms of God

their prejudices. Changing their point of view would be enough to get them to perceive a different shadow, and if they moved around more often they would notice that all these representations of God, the "little" God who is all that is accessible to them, are only images of the "big" God who is found outside, beyond their field of vision. "When one of them was freed and suddenly compelled to stand up, turn his head, walk and look up toward the light, he'd be pained and dazzled," Plato explains, and "if someone compelled him to look at the light itself, wouldn't his eyes hurt, and wouldn't he turn around and flee toward the things he's able to see . . . ?"[9]

Does God have a strategy? Now it seems to me that we can answer this question more easily. Is it a matter of the "little" God we can see or the "big" God we can only glimpse? To begin with, let us consider the first paradigm. God perhaps has a guideline, a direction. In his infinite power, in his eternity, it is hard for us to claim that he is letting the universe evolve by chance. At the very least, he has given it laws that govern it (the laws of mathematics and physics in particular, which appear to be universal). Still, if this guideline exists it is impossible for us to grasp it because God is incommensurable with us.

In the context of the second paradigm, the answer to our question is quite different. The strategy of God consists in protecting and promoting the people who are faithful to him within the context of a given religion. One can see how this strategy implies a direction, from which there necessarily follows a rule of common action. Given that the "little" God is a projection of the "big" God, whose being comprises an infinity of dimensions, the expression of this strategy and the rule of action that flows from it are strictly bound up with the religion to which they apply. Thus the strategy of God is different depending on whether you're looking at it from the standpoint of the Jewish, Catholic, or Muslim religion (or any other monotheist religion). As I said, by nature the God of the Jews protects Jews, the God of the Christians protects Christians, and the God of the Muslims protects Muslims. This explains how wars of religion can be waged by belligerents on both sides who take pride, *and rightly*, in a "true" vision of God, which constitutes *their* truth. Thus a crusade is a just war for Catholics; it is an offensive war approved and supported by God (by the "Catholic projection" of God in the context of the second paradigm). But to fight against the crusaders is equally a just war for Muslims: it is a defensive war approved

---

9. Ibid., 7:515c–e.

Does God Have a Strategy?

and supported by God (by the "Muslim projection" of God in the context of the second paradigm).

Since all these projections, all these revelations come about by the initiative of human beings, not God (the God of the first paradigm, of course), and since we cannot grasp the strategy of God inasmuch as he is "big," the question that arises is that of the validity of divine strategies in the context of the second paradigm. We have no assurance at all that these projections represent the will of God, for they are made at the level of our understanding, which is infinitely small. Thus as Catholics, we believe that a crusade is a just war. As Muslims, we believe that massacring as many infidel crusaders as possible is a just cause. Which is it, really? The answer to this question clearly does not lie in the domain of reason. It relies on guesswork, because the different religions are founded on different acts of faith, *which means different postulates.*

6
The God of Redemption

Phillip Cary—I want to be both more critical and more respectful of religion than I think you are suggesting. To explain why, let me say something about the concept of truth. I do not mean a concept like "their truth," as if Catholics have their truth and Muslims have their truth, and so on. No religion known to me makes truth claims of that sort. For that is not the concept of truth that is actually used in logic, science, or religion, all of which make a distinction between what people believe and what is true. People's beliefs can be true, but they can also be false. Hence there is no such thing as "their truth," except as a very misleading way of saying, "what they believe is true." For the important point is that what they believe is true may not be true.

Without this distinction between belief and truth, critical thought is impossible. And each of the great religions of the world, like all of the sciences, has a long tradition of engaging in critical thought about itself. That is what their theologies are about. They have not always succeeded in finding and believing the truth, but that has always been their aim. When, as sometimes happens, they merely insist on enforcing "their truth," then they have failed at their task.

So I want to respect the religions enough to say: they aim to believe the truth, not "their truth." As a religious person myself, I think I owe that much respect to other religions. But by the same token, I do not think we are doing anything alien to religious life when we think critically about the truth claims made by the religions.

Does God Have a Strategy?

The allegory of the cave is one of the most important moments in Western philosophy's attempt to understand how critical thinking is possible: how truth, not "our truth," can become the goal at which we aim, which actually guides and governs our critical inquiries even though it is a goal we never fully attain. For the point of Plato's allegory is that we do not have to remain chained by our prejudices. We can be freed: we can turn toward the light of the Good and climb out of the cave. The Good is the highest divinity, the ultimate Truth by which we judge. It is represented in the allegory by the sun that shines outside the cave, the supreme light by which the true forms of things can be seen, meaning especially the nature of goods such as virtue and justice and piety and wisdom. When someone like Socrates asks you critical questions about what justice is, this can make you uncomfortable (it "dazzles" and hurts your eyes) because it usually means discovering that your concept of justice—"your truth" about justice—is not really true. But precisely when you recognize that "your truth" is not true, you have taken a step toward the light. You have caught a glimpse of the true sun (not just the fire within the cave), because now you see more clearly by the light of the Good, and can discern what is not so good about your own concept of justice. And eventually, when you come back down to the cave, you will be able to think critically about all the shadows there. The shadows do imitate the form of higher goods; they are called by names like "justice" and "piety" and "wisdom" and so forth, and sometimes they are even good imitations of the true form of things. But they are never good enough, and always stand in need of critical investigation and correction. Thus we never possess the form of the Good itself (as if it was "our truth") but whenever we see clearly, we see by its light.

Behind the allegory of the cave is the Socratic practice of critical inquiry dramatized in Plato's dialogues, which is never satisfied with "our truth." Plato portrays Socrates inquiring about religion as well as politics, asking what piety really is as well as what justice really is. It is clear that Plato did not in fact believe the Greek myths about the "little" gods with their petty quarrels and deceit, and in the *Republic*, the long dialogue about justice that includes the allegory of the cave, he severely censors Greek mythology because he finds it unfit for instruction of the youth.[1] Any story about violent gods is to be expunged from the curriculum of education for children in his ideal, just city.

---

1. Plato, *Republic*, in *Complete Works*, 2:379a–383c.

6 – The God of Redemption

Plato also wrote a short dialogue in which Socrates has a conversation about piety with a self-satisfied humbug named Euthyphro. In this dialogue Socrates says quite explicitly that he cannot believe stories about gods fighting one another, such as when Zeus tied up his father, Cronus, who had earlier castrated his own father, Uranus.[2] Whatever strategy may be involved in such battles is surely unworthy of the gods! Yet these myths are "Euthyphro's truth," and it turns out Euthyphro is using them to justify a deadly attack he is making on his own father. If the gods can do it, then so can Euthyphro—it must be the pious thing to do! Socrates's conversation with Euthyphro is therefore Plato's attempt to deal with the way religion can become murderous, which I have been arguing is one of the key tasks of divine strategy as well. So it is worth seeing how this dialogue exemplifies the sort of critical thinking that Plato pictures for us in the allegory of the cave.

Euthyphro, we discover at the beginning of the dialogue, is prosecuting his father for murder. This is a capital crime in Athens, so Euthyphro's prosecution is in effect an attempt to kill his own father—a shocking and impious thing to do, on any ordinary view of piety. Socrates (who in one of the many ironies of the dialogue is quick to make friends with Euthyphro) is curious: does Euthyphro really think he knows so much about piety that he can dare to seek his father's life? Surely, most men could not do such a thing and think they are right, Socrates says, and adds (with an irony that Euthyphro entirely misses) that Euthyphro must surely know much more about piety than most men![3] Euthyphro agrees, for he is quite confident in "his truth" about piety. He is a prophet and soothsayer, and is convinced he is a very pious man who knows all about the subject. Indeed he is determined to kill his father for the sake of piety, and is happy to instruct Socrates about what piety is.

The ensuing conversation of course is rather comic. It soon becomes obvious that Euthyphro is not pious at all, knows nothing of what piety truly is, and does not know how to answer Socrates's questions about it. Any reader can see this, but the point is lost on Euthyphro, who never seems to notice Socrates's irony and keeps insisting on "his truth" about piety. After all, he is doing the same thing as Zeus and Cronus when they fought with their fathers! Here myth functions as murderous ideology, but it is comic because it is only the "truth" of one clueless old windbag who can do little harm (his case against his father is too obviously impious to

2. Plato, *Euthyphro*, in *Complete Works*, 6a.
3. Ibid., 4a.

Does God Have a Strategy?

be successful). But of course myths can function as "the truth" for a whole people, and then they can justify murder on a very large scale. At that point critical thinking in the spirit of Socrates, which might help us realize that "our truth" is not true, becomes a real service to the Good.

That is indeed one of the key points of the allegory of the cave. The main activity of those who remain in the cave is to compete in contests about who is best at naming the shadows and predicting their future course.[4] Soothsayers, we could call them, or prophets, preachers and priests, or else sophists and politicians and media consultants and marketing specialists. Being good at this game has its rewards, honor as well as wealth, and for a whole society the reward is the privilege of killing your enemies with the blessing of the gods—or for the sake of the Revolution, or Freedom and Democracy, or whatever ideology you believe in. This is how "our truth" works, when what matters is not what is true but what is accepted as true, what functions socially as truth. "Our truth" becomes part of a strategy of self-justification, power, and conquest. The point of the allegory of the cave is that if, unlike Euthyphro, we are willing to follow Socrates in asking critical questions, then we might at least hope to get free of "our truth" and see, in the light of the Good, what things really are true and good and just. And that might change life in the cave itself.

In fact I think it has. The spirit of Socrates has found its way into the best parts of Christianity, Judaism, and Islam, where it has met a spirit of prophecy that already belongs to those religions—a spirit that is capable, unlike Euthyphro, of critical thinking, including criticism of ideology and myth and justifications for murder. I think that even before their encounter with Socrates, all the great religions have resources within them for self-criticism and a place for critical questions, which is why the Abrahamic traditions in particular have a long history of critical interaction with Western philosophy. Among the heirs of Socrates are many Jews, Christians, and Muslims. So for example if you asked a Catholic priest today for his opinion about your statement that "*a crusade is a just war for Catholics*," I think you would find he disagreed with you.

This spirit of self-criticism, both prophetic and Socratic, is one reason I think the stories told about God in the Abrahamic traditions are different from pagan mythology. Although one can always find people in these traditions, Crusaders and their ilk, who treat their own religion the way Euthyphro treats the Greek myths, as justifications for their own murderousness,

---

4. Plato, *Republic*, in *Complete Works*, 7:516c; cf. 7:520c.

6 – The God of Redemption

I think we ought to expect better of them. This is part of treating religions with proper respect. I think Plato is right that we should judge religious beliefs in the light of the Good, which means we should reject as false and unjust any belief or piety or "truth"—especially in our own tradition—that actually promotes the kind of strategy you have described, in which God is imagined as a powerful being who will help us destroy our enemies if only we do what our priests tell us. As I said earlier, such a God would be a threat to the rest of humanity. And now I would add, just to be clear: the truth is that no such God exists. There can be no such thing as an evil and unjust God, the kind of God who is merely the strategist of one belligerent community against another. Such a God is not a truth of any kind—unless "truth" is put in scare-quotes as another way of saying "false belief."

The strategy of the God whose story is told in the Bible seems to me to be quite different, as I have been saying over the course of this conversation. In this strategy God chooses favorites such as Israel and Christ, who bless the world not by conquering it but by suffering in it. From this perspective the murderousness of human religions, including Christianity as well as Judaism and Islam, is one of the key challenges God's strategy must overcome, and the critical spirit of Socrates looks very much like an ally in this campaign.

Now to say something about what you call "the first paradigm" of divinity or what Plato called "the Good." Later Platonists called it also by the name "the One," and insisted very strongly, as you do, that it is incomprehensible, beyond any kind of understanding. They also were willing to say it is infinite, in the sense of unlimited, although more often they said it is *simple*, a technical term meaning that it has no parts, which means it also has no form, structure, or divisions. It was less like the set, "1, 2, 3, 4 ..., etc." than like a geometrical point, which contains no internal structure but from which all geometrical structures are derived. They would have liked your metaphor of "geometrical projections," I think, but would have insisted that complexity belongs only at this lower level of being, where the perfect simplicity and oneness of the Good unfolds in multiple projections or structures. The highest complexity they were willing to acknowledge was that of the divine Mind itself, filled with eternal forms of knowledge (including geometry, but also the eternal truth about justice, piety, wisdom, and so on). Although they did not take Greek mythology literally, they were happy to speak of a vast hierarchy of divinities, pure minds which emanated from the Good or the One, each an incomplete reflection of the highest principle at a lower level of being.

It is interesting what Christian Platonists like Augustine did with this set of ideas. Of course for them "the Good," the first principle of all, was another name for God. Another important Christian Platonist, called St. Denis by Catholics but "Pseudo-Dionysius" by modern scholars, added an interpretation of the Platonist hierarchy of divine minds, transforming it into the celestial hierarchy of angels. Both these thinkers came after the Council of Nicaea, which was the crucial event in church history that made it impossible for Christians to think of God himself as one of the "geometrical projections." The council and its aftermath, from which came the creed that is now recited in most churches every Sunday, ended up rejecting every attempt to say that Jesus Christ, as the Son of God, was a projection of the highest Good at a lower level, like one of those pure divine minds in the Platonist hierarchy that follows from the incomprehensible One. Instead, the council insisted that Christ is "true God from true God" and "of one being with the Father," which in the Platonist context of the time meant that he was none other than the Good itself.

Consequently, according to Nicene orthodoxy, everything that is said about the incomprehensibility of the Good or the One must be said also of Jesus Christ, because whatever is true of the divine being of God the Father is also true of the divine being of God the Son. Of course the human being of the Son when he becomes incarnate of the virgin Mary is different, for the Father is not God incarnate like the Son. But insofar as he is God, Jesus Christ belongs to what you have called the "first paradigm." That is what Christian orthodoxy, as represented by the Nicene Creed, is saying in the celebration of Christmas: this baby born of Mary is the highest and incomprehensible Good itself, the sun that shines above all things, which now dwells among us in the cave—not as an anthropomorphic god but as a man who is just as truly human as we are, and not as a projection of the divine but as the one true God, the incomprehensible source of all being.

This is the "both/and" I mentioned previously, which makes possible a divine strategy within the world of time and change. The chosen and favored one who blesses the world even in his suffering is the true God. As the church fathers have put it: remaining what he is, he takes up what he was not, so that our suffering and death become God's own. Therefore God is not the strategist of our murderousness but one who suffers from it, and only by suffering overcomes it.

6 – The God of Redemption

Jean-François Phelizon—Plato's allegory of the cave is fruitful indeed. The way we have transposed it, it affords us a grasp of the nature of God and the relativity of religions. Better yet, it affords us progress on the question that concerns us: "Does God have a strategy?" For in order to answer this question, it is obvious that we must first agree about the nature of God. It is for this purpose that I have introduced the two "paradigms."

Recall that the first paradigm corresponds to the God who is the creator of the universe, a God who is infinite in space, time, and complexity. Perhaps this God is only a concept, but it is a concept that *has* to be accepted, or else *no* religion can be considered true. The God of the second paradigm is the projection of the God of the first paradigm, a particular revelation of God that allows us to imagine him, to perceive him, to worship him, to pray to him within the context of a given religion. I called it a projection because, as we are unfortunately chained up in the cave, we can perceive only the shadow of divine reality—not the reality itself, which is found precisely outside the cave, which means beyond our reach and our understanding.

You write in reference to Plato that *"we should reject as false and unjust any belief or piety or 'truth' . . . that actually promotes the kind of strategy . . . in which God is imagined as a powerful being who will help us destroy our enemies if only we do what our priests tell us."* I thoroughly agree. That is the reason I am suspicious of every interpretation of God as *taking sides,* which is to say choosing one part of the human race over against another. This supposed choice seems to me strangely like a human invention.

But it does have to be acknowledged that this God who takes sides is an interpretation, not to say a faith, common to all three Abrahamic religions. The Old Testament is teeming with testimonies of God helping the Jewish people triumph over their enemies. In the same way, the Qur'an is full of references to God giving victory to the Muslims. Things are not the same in the New Testament, which is a message of justice and peace, but as we both pointed out earlier, numerous other texts need to be added to the four Gospels, the Epistles, and the book of Revelation in order to constitute Christian doctrine (which cannot be *reduced* to that of the New Testament). Many of these texts also put God on the side of Christians. And I need not mention the countless examples of Christians claiming that God was on their side to defeat their enemies, beginning with the preaching of the apostles, the first "missionaries."

Does God Have a Strategy?

The *church militant* is conscious of having received from Christ the fundamental obligation of being missionary. This obligation is established in the thinking of the first apostles: "As the Father has sent me, even so I am sending you," Jesus says to them in John 20:21, and "Go into all the world and proclaim the gospel to the whole creation" in Mark 16:15. It is true that today the church militant has lost some of its aggressiveness and its inspiration; it lacks precisely the apostles. It is no less true, as you rightly pointed out, that Catholic priests nowadays would not dare to claim that "a crusade is a just war."

But that's not how it was during the first nineteen centuries of the existence of Christianity. Need we be reminded that until the century of the Enlightenment, the church militant, in the name of which the Inquisition was established, assigned itself the strategy (I think we can use the word at this juncture) of doing whatever it takes, using whatever means necessary, to promote the *church triumphant*? The church triumphant thinks that the final victory belongs to Jesus Christ. It finds that the voices of the world, resounding with arrogance, cover up the witness of the apostles. But it believes that the Messiah will silence the "mouth speaking great things," for "his dominion is an everlasting dominion, which shall not pass away, and his kingdom is one that shall not be destroyed" (Dan 7:9, 14).

The notion of "just war" is thus not a special prerogative of the Muslim religion. It has also been extensively developed and utilized by the church. The church has become less aggressive in our day (it is even becoming pacifist) but there are still many cultural vestiges of the notion of just war in the contemporary Western world. Thus the invasion of Iraq was presented as a "just cause" by George W. Bush; likewise the French bombing of Libya was considered "just" by Nicolas Sarkozy and Bernard-Henri Lévy. In both cases, the horrors of war and the thousands of civilian victims were quite simply ignored. At a certain level of responsibility, no account is ever taken of what is euphemistically called "collateral damage."

So then, the God who takes sides and who keeps taking sides over the course of the centuries (and I repeat, this is the interpretation of God in the Abrahamic religions) has been (and could be again) the auxiliary of these particular religions and thus a threat to the others. Clearly such a God, because his sole strategy would be to defend a people or a religion *against* other peoples and religions, could not be considered completely "true." But this means that the image that we have made of God, as followers of a religion and prisoners of Plato's cave, is largely false because we interpret

6 – The God of Redemption

him in the light of the earthly and militant aspect of the religion to which we belong. At the very least, this image bears a troubling resemblance to ourselves. To me it seems to proceed from a conception of the divine that is as anthropomorphic as that of the Egyptians, the Greeks, or the Romans.

To be sure, one can claim that the church militant has distorted the original message we find in the Gospels, that it has taken advantage of it, even perverted it. For nowhere in the New Testament does it say that Christ came down to earth to confound the Jews, pagans, and infidels. It is still the orthodox view that the baby born of Mary *is* God, and that God dwells *within* the cave with Christians—not the God of Christians as a mere projection of God but, as you say, the "true God from true God." Unfortunately, reason puts this orthodoxy in the wrong.

To claim that Christ, chained with us in the cave, is actually the God of the first paradigm, really amounts to saying that there is no cave; that far from guessing at shadows, the human race stands fully in the light facing the infinite God. I don't share this interpretation. As I said before, to put man on exactly the same level as the God of the first paradigm is to vastly exaggerate the importance of the human species. In the face of God, how can such self-importance be accepted? I stick with the established fact, extensively corroborated by history, that the God of the second paradigm, the God in whom we believe if we still belong to one of the three Abrahamic religions, is rather an *interpretation* of the God of the first paradigm or, as I put it, a projection of the God of the first paradigm—a "true" projection for some because it is *revealed*, but false for others.

I turn now to the important assertion that *"God is not the strategist of our murderousness but one who suffers from it, and only by suffering overcomes it."* It seems to me that this discloses a new perspective on God, in the context of a *third paradigm* entirely contained within the New Testament and thus original, if I may say so, by comparison to the *doxa* of the other Abrahamic religions. The third paradigm is God not being able to bear the imperfections and sins of the human race but responding to the injustice and suffering in the world and assigning himself a mission: to redeem all humanity (and not just Christians). This is a new paradigm because God seems to be sorry for the existence of (a small) part of his work of creation: the human race. This is why he seeks to redeem them. (Conversely, he does not seem to be sorry for the rest of his creation because he does not assign himself the mission of redeeming other living beings nor yet of modifying in any way the universe he created.)

Does God Have a Strategy?

Note that our three paradigms refer to three different conceptions of the idea of God.

The first is philosophical: God is the principle of being and intelligibility, the ultimate reason of things, the *ratio ultima rerum*. Thus for Descartes, human reason is itself derived from divine reason. The veracity of God guarantees the truth of clear and distinct ideas. That is why in the *Discourse on Method* the exposition of Descartes's physics follows the proof for the existence of God. Properly speaking this conception of God is not religious, for God here is the foundation of the certainty of knowledge, and more broadly the principle of the unity of the universe.

The second conception is social and popular: as a product of the human imagination and its *tradition* from one generation to another, God is the guarantor of social unity. Durkheim claims that the idea of divinity stems from the idea of the sacred, via a process of personification and individualization, and that it is nothing other than the representation of society itself, raised to the status of a transcendent entity. Of course social cohesion nowadays appears more and more independent of any theological belief, but it was not always so. And the God of popular belief, as imagined by tradition or worshiped in the context of a religion, is still a center of collective unity and spiritual communion.

The third conception is moral and mystical: God is the source of the inner life. He is known by a feeling that is *sui generis*, deep in the unconscious regions of the mind, whose objective importance and philosophical interest, at the very least, is recognized by reason. We have seen there is a strong bond between the first two conceptions of God, in that the second is an accessible reduction of the first. The God of the metaphysicians is too distant, too ungraspable, above all too indifferent to answer the social needs of the religious sentiment; he has to be *humanized* somehow. Thus we see many thinkers sacrificing the infinitude of the metaphysical God for the sake of his religious value, his personal and moral character. But by losing his infinitude, God loses at the same time his *necessity*.

The bond between the mystical conception and the philosophical conception of God is on the other hand more difficult to establish. The one in fact claims to find God *within*, by a direct intuition or inner experience, while the other claims to find God *outwardly*, by a rational process; the God of Abraham, Isaac, and Jacob is *not* the God of the philosophers and the scholars, whose insufficiency Pascal experienced during his famous night of November 23, 1654.

6 – The God of Redemption

In any case, taking account of the third paradigm leads us back to our central question "Does God have a strategy?", which I would now like to approach from two slightly different angles.

1. An essential characteristic of strategy is that it is *never* risk-free. No strategy is certain; none is infallible. Because it is focused on the future, every strategy is necessarily endowed with a probability of success, which means it can fail. To be sure, the means which the strategist has at his disposal will, if used with skill and experience, increase the probability of victory, but not to the extent of making victory certain.

Since no strategy is infallible, this means that God, if he has a strategy, can be fallible. Here is something that contradicts the very nature of God. In regard to the first paradigm, it seems to me impossible to doubt the infallibility of God, given the infinity of his omnipotence. However, we have seen that we are incapable of establishing what his strategy might be. In regard to the second paradigm, in particular in the context of the Abrahamic religions, God is likewise infallible because he *is* the truth. This infallibility is found moreover in the certitudes of those who represent God on earth. The rabbi delivers and explains *the* truth (the word of God) to Jews, just as the priest (particularly the first among them, namely the pope) delivers *the* truth to Catholics, and the grand muftis, *the* truth to Muslims. In these three contexts, God guides those who worship him, leading them with certainty and assurance in a given direction—and thus he has a fixed and infallible strategy, which contradicts the very nature of strategy. Finally, in regard to the third paradigm, God has come down to earth. He has become man and is thus fallible. One can even affirm that he would normally make mistakes, except that his destiny is predetermined.

It seems Christians have gotten used to the simultaneous existence of the three paradigms: a God that is almighty, infinitely distant, the cause of fear, respect, and worship (coming from the Torah), a God that is astonishingly easy to influence, accessible to the mediation of the clergy (coming from Greco-Roman paganism) and a God that is strangely human, suffering from the injustices of this world, the basis of the submission of believers (coming from the New Testament). In Christian theology, these three paradigms complement each other. Yet the question of the infallibility of God is opposed to them.

But what *is* the strategy? For the sake of simplicity, let us limit ourselves to the Catholic religion (I could just as well have chosen the Jewish or Muslim religion). Every manifestation of a so-called divine strategy here

Does God Have a Strategy?

is the work of the church militant. It is the church that has introduced an element of uncertainty in the interpretation it gives us of God's intentions. As the future is not certain, providence does not provide for everything. So it grants free will to the believer. Nothing is gained for him: if he doesn't believe, if he is in a state of mortal sin at the moment he dies, then he is normally consigned to hell (which means, parenthetically, that Christ has not really come to save *all* humanity). In the name of this uncertainty, the church militant has been able to justify strategies of conquest—to conquer opinions by proselytizing as it has done over the centuries, and to conquer in a more earthly fashion through the wars of religion that have darkened the history of the Western world.

Need it be pointed out that in so doing the church militant has set itself apart from the founding message that Christ as man has come to bring deliverance to the earth, a message that is also strangely similar to that of the Buddha or Confucius? So should the God of the third paradigm simply be identified with the Buddha or Confucius? Should we follow Ernest Renan and consider only the extraordinary human qualities of Jesus? Should we deny the divine quality which Christians acknowledge in him? This is a question of interpretation, a question of faith that does not belong to the order of reason or of strategy.

2. A strategy is futile, or rather *it does not exist*, if the one who conducts it has no means of action at his disposal. So we also need to approach the question of divine strategy in relation to the means that are at God's disposal (or not) for carrying it out. Here again everything depends on which paradigm we consider.

It is clearly presumptuous to talk of the necessarily infinite means of the God of the first paradigm. Just as we can't know whether he has a strategy, we can't identify the means at his disposal. We know (or think we know) that the universe in which we live had a beginning (which does not mean that some other universe did not exist *before*). But we don't know if it will have an end, nor how it will end, nor *a fortiori* what will come *afterward*. We know also that humanity appeared on earth after a very, very long gestation (if the age of the earth is compared to a year, then the human species appeared less than four minutes before midnight on December 31), and that we are bound to disappear as a species, because like all living species we are dependent on the laws of biology. We can believe, but not prove, that the God of the first paradigm has favored the appearance of human beings on earth. However that may be, science teaches us more prosaically

6 – The God of Redemption

that we are the fruit of evolution, which means the result of chance. The existence of countless other inhabited worlds in the universe, which is now nearly certain, seems to confirm the hypothesis that the human species is at best an anomaly (in any case for us) at one point in space-time.

Looking now at the God of the second paradigm (the projection of God revealed to us by a religion) a divine strategy might exist, for we see that God has means to carry it out. In the Old Testament, God punishes and encourages the Jewish people, he inspires the prophets, he gives victory to David. He is near to the Jewish people he has chosen (but not to the human race in general) and he seems to have at his disposal a variety of means for protecting his people, which he puts to use on condition that the Jewish people don't give themselves over to idolatry. For Christians also, the God of the second paradigm is near. The person of faith *hears* him and *feels his presence*. The voices of Joan of Arc, the ecstasies of Bernadette of Lourdes, are direct manifestations of God, just like all the miracles he does. So God is not bereft of means, though he nonetheless does not give the impression of carrying out a precise strategy.

I said just now that the church militant has carried out many temporal actions in the name of God, disposing of every means that is humanly imaginable. Yet the result of these actions on earth is not conclusive at this point, because the church militant has not become universal. So everything happens as if God were strikingly lacking in means. He does not even seem capable of reducing the misery, injustice, and suffering of humans or animals, or of bringing peace to the human groups that keep killing each other for the most pointless motive of all: to impose *their* truth on other human groups.

This rather bitter fact of the powerlessness of the God of the second paradigm is just as valid for Islam. The Qur'an has a great deal to tell us about the tricks God uses to outmaneuver the human race. It doesn't tell us why. It warns Muslims that all their words are heard, all their actions scrutinized; it even threatens them with thunderbolts from hell. But these threats do not constitute means for *elevating* Muslims. They function, rather, in the manner of biblical commandments or threats of excommunication that are in force in the Catholic Church, as reminders of discipline, of what one *must* believe and how one *must* act.

Thus within the three Abrahamic religions, the means attributed to God are no different from the earthly means of the religions. This renders suspect the very existence of a divine strategy. For, however almighty at a

Does God Have a Strategy?

conceptual level, God shows he is essentially powerless when it comes to directing the affairs of this world. To be sure, he seems to influence the conscience of human beings—at least we may hope so. But does the human conscience need God to construct a morality, to know what is right, to recognize the best interests of the human race? No—and the proof is that the religions that do not acknowledge the God of the second paradigm (I am referring particularly to the religions of Asia) are not missing anything by way of morality in comparison to the Abrahamic religions.

This powerlessness of God is yet more flagrant if one considers the third paradigm. If we actually accept that God has come down to earth to redeem the human race, to suffer with it, then we should also accept that God is powerless to elevate us and that though he is undoubtedly compassionate toward the imperfect creatures he has created, he unfortunately cannot change them, improve them, or make them holy (of course I am setting aside a few exceptions).

Thus I would say schematically that the God of the first paradigm may have a strategy and at any rate has the means to carry it out; that the God of the second paradigm, as a projection of the first, has means at his disposal to influence his followers (at least that's what they believe) but that apart from affirming that the militancy of the religions is not in essence a human phenomenon, he is singularly lacking a credible strategy; that the God of the third paradigm, who is certainly compassionate, is content with messages of a moral order, messages that are noble and enthusiastic ("Love one another" is not too bad as a *new* testament) but messages that are, alas, bereft of real effect on the situation of the human race. It is in the context of the third paradigm that a divine strategy most seems to be missing at the operational level.

Phillip Cary—It seems that now is the time to talk about the weakness of God. This is an important theme connected to the Christian doctrine of incarnation, a theme that is brought out with particular clarity by our question, "Does God have a strategy?" For if God has a strategy then he must be faced with threats and dangers, as well as the prospect of failure and mischance in a world where nothing is certain. It is helpful when you sum up the issues that arise here under the heading of redemption, God's strategy for "buying back" his creation. (In English the connection between redeeming and buying back is not quite as explicit as in French, where *racheter* is the verb for both.)

6 – The God of Redemption

The God of redemption belongs to what you call the third paradigm, in contrast to the God of the first paradigm, the infinite and incomprehensible God. Of course as a Christian, I believe there is only one God, so I will treat these two paradigms as two different ways of talking about one and the same God. I take the second paradigm to be a destructive human fantasy that deserves the name "paganism," but which can easily—indeed, with frightening ease—become the strategy of any community or group. It is the strategy of those I called, at the beginning of our discussion, the "recalcitrant others" with whom God's strategy must deal. The first and the third paradigms, on the contrary, I think are both forms of human discourse that can be used to say something true about one and the same God, though it is sometimes hard to see how both can be true at the same time. But this is the both/and to which the doctrine of incarnation commits us, if we are orthodox Christians—by which I mean not only Roman Catholics but Eastern Orthodox and also Protestants, such as myself.

I should mention that not every aspect of your notion of the third paradigm interests me. I have devoted a fair amount of my own scholarly work to showing that the idea of finding God *within*, in a direct intuition or inner experience, is originally a metaphysical notion stemming from Augustine's Platonism. Western mysticism in general, I think, has deep roots in the pagan Neoplatonism of Plotinus, who is one of the main inspirations for Augustinian inwardness. So I think mysticism and philosophy go hand in hand, and I am interested in looking elsewhere for redemption. I think we meet God the way we meet other persons, and we don't find other persons by looking inside ourselves. We find them in their own flesh, which is external to us (indeed, there is nothing more "external" than flesh). So I look for redemption in a God who meets us "outwardly," in human flesh, by making our weakness his own.

The notion of redemption appears in both Judaism and Christianity, though it is a particularly intense focus of Christian thought. To talk about God redeeming the world is a favorite Christian way of articulating what I earlier described as God's strategy for blessing the world. It is the strategy of one who has apparently suffered an initial defeat: captives are redeemed by buying them back from an enemy who has captured them. According to Christian theology, the blood of Christ is the price of the ransom paid by God to redeem his creation from the power of evil, which has won an initial victory. It is a strategy for reclaiming what is his own, restoring his

Does God Have a Strategy?

own creation to the blessing and happiness that he had always intended for it. But it is also part of an overarching strategy of battle.

It is an odd strategy, because God appears to keep losing. This is why I think it is important to talk about the weakness of God. According to the doctrine of the incarnation, the God of the first paradigm, whose providence oversees all the events of history, is also the baby born in the manger on Christmas day, who must suckle at his mother's breast or he will die, who barely escapes the attempts of King Herod to kill him, and who some thirty-odd years later does not escape being executed by Pontius Pilate. Could it be that God's strategy has encountered an unexpected defeat at this point? Of course, Christian theology answers no, and it is precisely at this point that the Bible speaks of divine foreknowledge and even predestination, saying that Jesus was handed over to death "according to the definite plan and foreknowledge of God" (Acts 2:23), in order to emphasize in the most unmistakable terms that the infinite God who controls all events in history has not been defeated in this event of crucifixion, which is the death of his own Son.

The usual metaphysics that Christian theologians use to account for the possibility of this odd strategy refers to two different orders or levels of causality, which are characteristic of the first and third paradigms. There is a primary causality that belongs to God alone as the Creator and First Cause of all things, and then there are numerous secondary causes, including all physical causes as well as human free wills. The two orders of causality operate in different dimensions, but intersect. Traditionally, they are thought of as vertical and horizontal.

If you compare all of history to a timeline, then the Creator is above the whole line and can see all of it at once: everything that we call past, present, and future. That is divine "foreknowledge," though strictly speaking it is an eternal knowledge of past, present and future together. As Thomas Aquinas explains, it is not like someone traveling along a road, who cannot see those who are far ahead of him—that's our situation—but rather like someone looking down on the whole road from a great height, who can see its beginning, middle, and end all in one glance.[5] Thus God sees in one simple act of knowledge all things that exist at any point in time.

Now change the image slightly: imagine God *underneath* the timeline, supporting it at every point, because unless he held it up, it would fall into nonbeing. This is the "vertical" dimension of primary causality, which

---

5. Aquinas, *Summa Theologica*, I, 14.13, reply to objection 3.

6 – The God of Redemption

is the power of the Creator to give being and power to all things. The reason there are secondary causes operating and having an effect "horizontally" is because they are created, given being and power by the First Cause. Like the divine knowledge, which sees all of time "in one glance," the First Cause is simple, not complex: it gives being to the whole creation, past, present, and future, in one act. (Imagine the whole timeline bent in a circle around a central point, and resting all its weight directly on that one simple point).

This is only a picture, of course, but it is meant to illustrate some concepts that Christian theology has adapted from the Western metaphysical tradition stemming from Plato. First of all, the vertical kind of causality does not work the same way as the horizontal causality. They are not in competition with one another. At the horizontal level, I can push you and you can pull me, and we can have rival strategies and try to outwit or defeat one another. But the vertical causality of God is never part of that kind of battle. It always *gives* being and power and knowledge, never takes it away, for it is not in competition with our power but is the source of it. It is an infinite and inexhaustible source, and nothing we do can limit or diminish its power. We can only benefit from it, not fight it.

So at the level of primary causality (or what you are calling the first paradigm) there is no real possibility of strategy, because God is simply too powerful for that. This is not because he has *more* power than the secondary causes he has created, as if the two kinds of power could be measured on the same scale. (They are in the strict sense incommensurable, which means precisely: not measurable on the same scale.) Rather, he has an entirely different kind of power. Created things can never put up any resistance to his power, not because he overpowers them, but because the two kinds of power or causality are not operating in the same dimension. It would be like saying: if I push hard enough, I can force two and two to make five. To think that way is simply to misunderstand the nature of causality.

So there is never a battle between God and his creatures at the level of primary causality, where there is no logical possibility of resistance or competition or strategy. No stratagem of ours could ever have an effect on God. For the same reason there is no possibility of God, as First Cause, ever using means, something less powerful than he is, in order to accomplish his purposes. Means can fail us, in this world full of recalcitrant others, for our means too can be recalcitrant, not perfectly suited to our purposes. Such imperfection and failure is simply impossible for the Cause that gives being and power to all things, including every means used by his creatures.

Does God Have a Strategy?

So God has a strategy only because he has chosen to become something more—which is the same as to say, something less—than the omnipotent First Cause that created all things. This is where Christian theology moves decisively beyond Platonist philosophy. According to the Christian doctrine of incarnation, God has chosen to enter the world he created as one creature among others, one secondary cause among others—by becoming one person among others, the man Jesus Christ. This is the weakness of God. It means, inevitably, that among all the secondary causes of the world he must choose some means rather than others, because he has dangers to face and obstacles to overcome. And he must face uncertainty, because no one who uses means in a world of competing forces is sure to succeed. And in order to become a person among other persons he must become a member of one particular people; so he takes sides in their battles and he shares in their strategy. For example, he speaks to his disciples—all of them Jews, remember—about their hope for a king, a Messiah who will free the Jewish people from their Roman conquerors, and he warns them of destruction and judgment, because he is himself a very different kind of king from what they expected (Matt 24).

In short, the weakness of God, which alone makes divine strategy possible, stems from his becoming, in the incarnation, a secondary cause as well as the primary cause. Having become one of us, using means like us, he can fight with us, strategize with us and also against us. He is subjected to all the uncertainties of mortal life and its battles. And he can lose. He can suffer and die. But he can also win the fight—something impossible to the First Cause in itself, which has no battles to fight.

The question then is: what kind of battle is he fighting? We need to ask not only whether God has a strategy but what his strategy is. And this is why I keep saying his strategy is odd. He is not like a general leading troops into battle and trying to defeat an enemy. He is trying *to redeem his enemies.* He wins the battle by suffering and dying, and then defeating death itself in his own person by virtue of being raised from the dead. Such at least is the Christian gospel.

It is odd, but I think it is the kind of thing we should expect, once we understand why no version of the second paradigm could possibly be true. It cannot be that God, the First Cause, should ever confront us as one vastly more powerful than we are, like the gods of the second paradigm. For merely to have *more* power than we have—no matter how much more—is to have the same *kind* of power as we have, a power commensurable with

6 – The God of Redemption

that of his creatures, which means to have a far less effective power than the omnipotence of the First Cause. There is no reason why the omnipotent Creator would adopt so meager a power as his own creatures, unless the whole point were for him to become powerless: to be able to fail, to suffer and to die. And that, again, is the Christian gospel, the good news about the divine strategy: he became weak so that we might become strong, he became mortal so that we might have everlasting life, he became one of the defeated of this world so that the afflicted and oppressed might have hope.

This means also that the strategy of God's people cannot possibly be one of conquest in any literal sense. The church militant is not like an ordinary army out to defeat its opponents. Its task is to bear witness to the God who came among us, as it were incognito, looking very much like a failure who was crucified, dead, and buried. And that means the great stratagem of the Christian faith is to share in Christ's sufferings. Hence it is no accident that the Greek word for witness, *martyros*, became our word for martyr. The soldiers of Christ are those who, like their master, bear witness to the goodness of God even to the point of death. That is how they fight the good fight. Any time they lapse into thinking of God in the way of the second paradigm, where God is a big powerful guy who destroys their enemies—an imaginary power that is the projection not of the omnipotent Creator but of our own murderousness—they start behaving like pagans, failing to bear faithful witness to the odd strategy of the God who became weak in order to redeem his enemies.

Jean-François Phelizon—I'm going to take up some of our conclusions about the first two paradigms and develop them further. I suggest to you that by doing so one can arrive at the third paradigm, which appears to me to be completely different in nature.

It seems to me we are largely in agreement about the nature of God as far the first paradigm is concerned: he is incommensurable, ungraspable, unattainable, incomprehensible to our understanding. Worse yet, *he is infinitely distant, which means he is infinitely absent* for us others, human beings. We can imagine his existence, we can believe he exists, that he is true, but we cannot communicate with him; he cannot talk with us, or more precisely, we couldn't understand him if he did. As a result, we cannot even call out to him. As you have noted, the God of the first paradigm is the one the Deists believed in, beginning with Aristotle, for whom God is the "First Mover," not necessarily conscious or endowed with reason, who

Does God Have a Strategy?

constitutes the reason for every movement in the universe. The God of the first paradigm is also the supreme Being celebrated by Voltaire, as well as the one that unfortunately inspired Robespierre to found his (fortunately) short-lived cult.

Let us reread a bit of Voltaire. For him, the true Deist

> is a man firmly convinced of the existence of a supreme being as good as he is powerful, who has created all extended, vegetating, sentient and thinking beings, who perpetuates their species, who punishes crimes without cruelty, and benevolently rewards virtuous behaviour.... United in this principle with the rest of the universe, he does not embrace any of the sects, which all contradict each other. His religion is the most ancient and the most widespread, for the simple worship of one god preceded all the world's systems. He speaks a language all peoples understand though they do not understand one another. He has brothers from Peking to Cayenne, counting all wise men as his brothers. He holds that religion consists neither in the opinions of an unintelligible metaphysics nor in a vain apparatus, but in worship and justice. To do good, that is his cult. To submit to god, that is his doctrine. The Mohammedan cries out to him: "take care if you don't make the pilgrimage to Mecca!" "Woe to you," he is told by a Recollet, "if you don't make the journey to our lady of Loretto!" He laughs at Loretto and Mecca, but he helps the poor and he defends the oppressed."[6]

When it comes to the strategy of this supreme Being, we know nothing. François Quesnay put it quite well: Human beings cannot penetrate the designs of the supreme being in the construction of the universe. They cannot rise to the level of knowing the immutable rules that he has instituted for the formation and conservation of his work. Indeed, we are incapable of knowing whether the universe has a meaning, because we do not positively know whether God exists. We will never know whether the universe has always existed or whether it was created. And if it was created, we will never know whether it was created with a particular purpose.

Suppose the God of the first paradigm created the universe and that the universe is the whole of what exists. Then before the creation of the world, God existed and the universe did not; afterwards, God and the universe coexist. But with God as part of the universe, which is the whole of what exists, he could not exist before the creation of the world, which

---

6. Voltaire, *Philosophical Dictionary*, 386.

6 – The God of Redemption

contradicts our supposition. Yet we cannot infer just from this contradiction that God doesn't exist.

Suppose now that God, creator of the universe, is *not* part of the universe, which means the universe is the whole of what exists, except for God. The same problem presents itself at a higher level if we consider the "super universe" composed of God and the universe he has created. Has this super universe always existed or was it created? If it was created, then by whom? What is this "super God" that has created God? Of course, one could extend this paradox of the *mise en abyme* of the universe indefinitely, again without ever succeeding in proving that he exists or that he doesn't.

These contradictions and paradoxes necessarily leave us guessing. I repeat that the God of the first paradigm is incommensurable; we cannot affirm anything about his existence and influence, much less his strategy. We cannot put ourselves "at his level," and the reverse is probably true as well. Nor have the three Abrahamic religions gotten us past the guesses and resolved the paradox of the *mise en abyme*. To be sure, they affirm that God exists. But they stop well short of explaining whether God is part of the universe or not.

Let us now reread Genesis, because it ventures to describe the creation of the world: "In the beginning, God created the heavens and the earth. And the earth was without form and void, and darkness was over the face of the deep. And the Spirit of God was hovering over the face of the waters. And God said 'Let there be light,' and there was light. And God saw that the light was good. And God separated the light from the darkness. God called the light Day, and the darkness he called Night. And there was evening and there was morning, the first day" (Gen 1:1-5). The Bible presents us with a poetic and moving image of the creation of the earth, but not of the universe (which had already existed for nine billion years before the appearance of the solar system). The God who created the earth (and not the universe) is not the God of the first paradigm but rather that of the second paradigm, i.e., a projection of the supreme Being *limited* to the planet where the human species made its appearance.

Thus concerning the first paradigm we can say that something absolutely surpasses us in this world; that there are forces around us which perhaps do not operate at random; that there are worlds we will never know and an earth, not to mention the universe, that will survive the human species. And we are certain that solar system will come to an end long before the end of the universe. But we cannot say anything as to the power of the

Does God Have a Strategy?

forces that absolutely surpass us nor anything as to the actual strategy of the supreme Being, because he is (as I said) infinitely absent. That's why I cannot but subscribe to what you have written: "*It cannot be that God, the First Cause, should ever confront us as one vastly more powerful than we are, like the gods of the second paradigm. For merely to have more power than us—no matter how much more—is to have the same kind of power as we have, a power commensurable with that of his creatures.*"

You associate the God of the second paradigm, the projection or revelation of the supreme Being in the context of a monotheist religion, with paganism. "*I take the second paradigm to be a destructive human fantasy that deserves the name 'paganism,' but which can easily—indeed, with frightening ease—become the strategy of any community or group.*" The term *paganism* is interesting because it *trivializes* certain practices of the monotheist religions. It confuses them, if I may say so, with the practices of all the other religions, for example the religions of Asia. Yet it is indeed God who appears throughout the sacred texts of the Old Testament and the Qur'an (let us set the Gospels aside for a moment). It is indeed the God of the second paradigm, insofar as he is a projection or a revelation of the supreme Being, whom Jews and Muslims reverence by means of these texts.

But this projection is not exempt from transformations and distortions. Because the God of the second paradigm is an image of God as seen by human beings, it is perfectly typical that he shows up as the supreme leader of the monotheist religions. He is of course superior to human beings, but not so much so that he cannot help, guide, direct, and judge them. *Thus, in contrast to the God of the first paradigm, who is infinitely absent, the God of the second paradigm is strikingly present.* That is why, as we shall see, he is transformed quite naturally into a warlord. Here we have a "frightening" paradox, in your own terms, because the "sacred" texts—whichever ones—make an absolute demand of fidelity, the apparent source of intolerance, which they express in correlation with repeated threats against the infidel. Is this not proof of their all-too-human character?

God as warlord, *chef de guerre*: this is how the spiritual gives way to the temporal. In fact paganism arises within a religion (in other words, a religion become "pagan") when the projection it makes of God is turned to the profit of a given group of individuals, or when the invocation of God starts to serve particular material interests. Wherever religion appears, Proudhon observed, it is not as an organizing principle, but as a means of gaining mastery over wills. With paganism, a strategy can start to be

6 – The God of Redemption

established, a human strategy carried out in the name of God but identified with the divine strategy, even if it violates the most basic ethics. One can understand why sacred texts justify war and make apologias for it: this is an *instrumentalization* of God in the context of the second paradigm. God *ought* to serve those who are faithful to him; he *ought* to contribute to justifying war. In this all-too-human context, it is normal for God to take sides, to fight on behalf of the agonistic community of the faithful, since he is their leader and is thought to guide them.

In this sense, what do we find in this regard in the Old Testament and the Qur'an (I deliberately continue to leave the Gospels aside)? Let's start with the Old Testament.

To begin with, it's necessary to prepare for war: "Proclaim this among the nations: Consecrate for war, stir up the mighty men. Let all the men of war draw near, let them come up. Beat your plowshares into swords, and your pruning hooks into spears" (Joel 3:9–10).

For it's a matter of resolutely waging war in the name of God—"Cursed is he who does the work of the LORD with slackness and cursed is he who keeps back his sword from bloodshed" (Jer 48:10)—without hesitating to massacre every one of the enemy: "But in the cities of these peoples that the LORD your God is giving you for an inheritance, you shall save alive nothing that breathes" (Deut 26:10); "And Joshua overwhelmed Amalek and his people with the sword. Then the LORD said to Moses, 'Write this as a memorial in a book and recite it in the ears of Joshua, that I will utterly blot out the memory of Amalek from under heaven'" (Exod 17:13–14). "And the LORD routed Sisera and all his chariots and all his army before Barak by the edge of the sword. And Sisera got down from his chariot and fled away on foot. And Barak pursued the chariots and the army to Harosheth-hagoyim, and all the army of Sisera fell by the edge of the sword; not a man was left" (Judg 4:15–16). "And Gaal went out at the head of the leaders of Shechem and fought with Abimelech. And Abimelech chased him, and he fled before him. And many fell wounded, up to the entrance of the gate. . . . And Abimelech fought against the city all that day. He captured the city and killed the people who were in it, and he razed the city and sowed it with salt" (Judg 9:39–45). "Thus says the LORD of hosts: 'I have noted what Amalek did to Israel in opposing them on the way when they came up out of Egypt. Now go and strike Amalek and devote to destruction all that they have. Do not spare them, but kill both man and woman, child and infant, ox and sheep, camel and donkey" (1 Sam 15:2–3). "The LORD, the God of

Does God Have a Strategy?

their fathers . . . brought up against them the king of the Chaldeans, who killed their young men with the sword in the house of their sanctuary and had no compassion on young man or virgin, old man or aged. He gave them all into his hand" (2 Chr 36:15–17).

One could of course multiply examples. See for instance how Joshua massacres all the inhabitants of the cities of Makkedah, Libnah, Lachish, Eglon, Hebron, and Debir (Josh 10:28–39): "He left none remaining, but devoted to destruction all that breathed, just as the Lord God of Israel commanded . . . because the Lord God of Israel fought for Israel" (Josh 10:40–42).

War waged under the invocation of God does not exclude pillage (in this sense, it is *normal*): "So the people [of Israel] shouted and the trumpets were blown. As soon as the people heard the sound of the trumpet, the people shouted a great shout, and the wall fell down flat, so that the people went up into the city, every man straight before him, and they captured the city. Then they devoted all in the city to destruction, both men and women, young and old, oxen, sheep and donkeys, with the edge of the sword" (Josh 6:17–21). "If [the city] makes no peace with you, but makes war against you, then you shall besiege it. And when the Lord your God gives it into your hand, you shall put all its males to the sword, but the women and the little ones, the livestock, and everything else in the city, all its spoil, you shall take as plunder for yourselves. And you shall enjoy the spoil of your enemies, which the Lord your God has given you" (Deut 20:12–14). "And [Saul] took Agag the king of the Amalekites alive and devoted to destruction all the people with the edge of the sword. But Saul and the troops spared Agag and the best of the sheep and of the oxen and of the fattened calves and the lambs, and all that was good, and would not utterly destroy them. All that was despised and worthless they devoted to destruction" (1 Sam 15:8–9). "And the people of Israel took captive the women of Midian and their little ones, and they took as plunder all their cattle, their flocks, and all their goods. All their cities in the places where they lived, and all their encampments, they burned with fire, and took all the spoil and all the plunder, both of man and of beast. Then they brought the captives and the plunder and the spoil to Moses, and to Eleazar the priest, and to the congregation of the people of Israel, at the camp on the plains of Moab by the Jordan at Jericho" (Num 31:9–13). "The men of Israel took captive 200,000 of their relatives, women, sons and daughters. They also took much spoil from them and brought the spoil to Samaria" (2 Chr 28:8). "And Moses was

6 – The God of Redemption

angry with the officers of the army, the commanders of thousands and the commanders of hundreds, who had come from service in the war. Moses said to them, 'Have you let all the women live? Behold, these, on Balaam's advice, caused the people of Israel to act treacherously against the LORD in the incident of Peor, and so the plague came among the congregation of the LORD. Now therefore, kill every male among the little ones, and kill every woman who has known man by lying with him. But all the young girls who have not known man by lying with him keep alive for yourselves" (Num 31:14–18).

Of course, I am not maintaining in any way that the Bible contains nothing but massacres—quite the contrary. I simply want to show that the God of the second paradigm, transformed by the human imagination, can appear even in sacred texts as a ferocious and determined warlord.

If we open the Qur'an, we find the same kind of transformation. There God is represented at great length as an inflexible warlord. Thus: "Let those fight in the way of Allah who sell the life of this world for the other. Whoso fighteth in the way of Allah, be he slain or be he victorious, on him We shall bestow a vast reward" (4:74). "Hast thou not seen those unto whom it was said: Withhold your hands, establish worship and pay the poor-due, but when fighting was prescribed for them behold! a party of them fear mankind even as their fear of Allah or with greater fear, and say: Our Lord! Why hast thou ordained fighting for us? If only Thou wouldst give us respite yet a while! Say (unto them, O Muhammad): The comfort of this world is scant; the Hereafter will be better for him who wardeth off (evil); and ye will not be wronged the down upon a date-stone" (4:77). "So fight (O Muhammad) in the way of Allah—Thou art not taxed (with the responsibility for anyone) except for thyself—and urge on the believers. Peradventure Allah will restrain the might of those who disbelieve. Allah is stronger in might and stronger in inflicting punishment" (4:84). "They long that ye should disbelieve even as they disbelieve, that ye may be upon a level (with them). So choose not friends from them till they forsake their homes in the way of Allah; if they turn back (to enmity) then take them and kill them wherever ye find them, and choose no friend nor helper from among them" (4:89). "Ye will find others who desire that they should have security from you, and security from their own folk. So often as they are returned to hostility they are plunged therein. If they keep not aloof from you nor offer you peace nor hold their hands, then take them and kill them wherever ye find them. Against such We have given you clear warrant" (4:91).

Does God Have a Strategy?

And again: "Those of the believers who sit still, other than those who have a (disabling) hurt, are not on an equality with those who strive in the way of Allah with their wealth and lives. Allah hath conferred on those who strive with their wealth and lives a rank above the sedentary. Unto each Allah hath promised good, but he hath bestowed on those who strive a great reward above the sedentary" (4:95). "The only reward of those who make war upon Allah and his messenger and strive after corruption in the land will be that they will be killed or crucified, or have their hands and feet on alternate sides cut off, or will be expelled out of the land. Such will be their degradation in the world, and in the Hereafter theirs will be an awful doom" (5:33).

Furthermore, it is worth explaining the necessary and sufficient conditions that make joining in *jihad* ("holy war" and therefore just war) an obligation for Muslims. There are four separate conditions: when non-Muslims enter or invade Muslim territory, when battle lines begin to draw near, when the imam calls a person or a people to go into battle, or when non-Muslims capture and imprison a group of Muslims. Thus: "Sanction is given unto those who fight because they have been wronged; and Allah is indeed able to give them victory; those who have been driven from their homes unjustly only because they said: Our Lord is Allah" (Qur'an 22:39–40). "If the enemy enters a Muslim country, there is no doubt that it is obligatory for those in countries on its borders to defend it. If they are lazy or incapable, then the mobilization proceeds to those in surrounding countries, and then in turn to those surrounding them, until it embraces the whole world, East and West, because Muslim countries form one sole country."[7] "Whoever knows of the weakness of Muslims in the face of their enemies, and knows that he can reach them and help them, has the duty also of going into battle."[8]

As the famous Muslim historian Ibn Khaldun (1332–1406) writes in *The Muqaddimah*: "In the Muslim community, the holy war [*jihad*] is a religious duty, because of the universalism of the (Muslim) mission and (the obligation to) convert everybody to Islam either by persuasion or by force. . . . The other religious groups did not have a universal mission and the holy war was not a religious duty to them, save only for purposes of

---

7. Ibn Taymiyya, *Majmu Al-Fatawa*, vol. 28.
8. Al-Qurtubi, *Fath-ul-Bari*, 6/30.

6 – The God of Redemption

defense." Hence unlike other religious groups, Islam is "under obligation to gain power over other nations."[9]

The reasons for waging *jihad* are thus very extensive. However, they do not go so far as to justify certain extreme measures such as terrorist actions. These are in fact severely condemned by the authorities of Islam, based on the prohibition of killing the innocent: "whoso killeth a human being for other than manslaughter or corruption in the earth, it shall be as if he had killed all mankind" (Qur'an 5:32). There is also the prohibition against provoking chaos (*al fitnah*), which is "worse than slaughter. And fight not with them at the Inviolable Place of Worship until they first attack you there, but if they attack you (there) then slay them. Such is the reward of disbelievers" (Qur'an 2:191). And there is the absolute condemnation of suicide (Qur'an 4:29). Nonetheless it is also worth noting the following verse in the Qur'an concerning the relation between Muslims and infidels: "We have done with you. And there hath arisen between us and you hostility and hate forever until ye believe in Allah only" (Qur'an 60:4).

Here again, I am not at all maintaining that the Qur'an is inciting war; I simply want to show how the God of the second paradigm can be transformed into a warlord. I quite admire the Muslim concept that forbids representing God in human form. This contrasts with the Christian concept: "Previously God, who has neither a body nor a face, absolutely could not be represented by an image. But now that he has made himself visible in the flesh [in Christ] and has lived with men, I can make an image of what I have seen of God."[10]

But as we have just seen, this prohibition applies to *images,* not at all to *writings,* where God by contrast takes on the traits of an authoritarian general—far from the promise made elsewhere to believers: "Allah tasketh not a soul beyond its scope" (Qur'an 2:286).

We have seen how, in two of the three Abrahamic religions, the projection of God can be instrumentalized by human beings. There is in fact a huge gap between the initial messages (for these religions really do bear messages of peace) and the reality of history.

As a result of this instrumentalization of God, many wars have been justified in his name. Thus the God of the second paradigm, who was in the beginning essentially spiritual, becomes a first-rate auxiliary to the real warlords of every era. And still today, the human race has not given up

---

9. Ibn Khaldun, *Muqaddimah*, vol. 1, 473.
10. *Catechism of the Catholic Church*, §1159, quoting St. John of Damascus.

Does God Have a Strategy?

taking advantage of the image it has of God in order to develop, as you say, its "destructive human fantasies." That's why you are right to explain that "*The soldiers of Christ are those who, like their master, bear witness to the goodness of God. . . . Any time they lapse into thinking of God in the way of the second paradigm, where God is a big powerful guy who destroys their enemies—an imaginary power that is the projection not of the omnipotent Creator but of our own murderousness—they start behaving like pagans.*"

So we can say that the God of the second paradigm, as represented by the monotheist religions, then distorted and transformed by them, does indeed have a strategy. Or more precisely that he gives the impression of having a strategy, generally more operational than conceptual. Unfortunately this strategy, which serves primarily temporal interests, is all too human, as attested by countless historical examples. "All mysticism degenerates into politics," as Charles Péguy lucidly puts it.

That being so, what about the God of the third paradigm? I said earlier that this was quite a different subject. That's what we need to delve into now, not only on the basis of the Gospels, but also on the basis of what Christians have done with them up to now.

7

Jesus and the Church in History

Phillip Cary—It is time for me to sum up what I want to say about your three paradigms. It is especially important at this point to make clear where I disagree.

First of all, I do not think there is any such thing as "the God of the first paradigm" or "the God of the second paradigm" and so on. There is only one God, and the three paradigms are at best three different types of discourse used to describe him. And sometimes they misdescribe him, which is to say that sometimes what they say is not true. That's where our disagreements come in.

As you suggested, we probably disagree least about the first paradigm. I would call this type of discourse the metaphysics of God. It draws its conceptual resources from the classical philosophical tradition, especially Platonism, but it has long been a native part of the theological traditions of Judaism, Christianity, and Islam. Here I will give you some ways that a rather standard Christian metaphysics (say, that of the great Catholic theologian Thomas Aquinas) would disagree with what you say about "the God of the first paradigm."

It belongs to the metaphysics of God, for example, to describe divine transcendence in ways that don't get caught in the *mise en abyme* you describe. Just as the Good never becomes our possession ("our truth") but is always the light beyond us by which we judge and critique whatever truth we believe we possess, so also the being of God is never one being among others, as if God were just one more item we could put on our list of all the things that exist. Therefore God is not part of the universe, nor can he be set beside the universe as if it were one thing and he were another, so that both together form a "super universe." To describe God's being that way is to misdescribe it. He is not "a being" in any ordinary sense of the word. It is better to say he is "above being," like the prominent strand of Christian Neoplatonism stemming from Pseudo-Dionysius (known to the tradition as St. Denis).

When you try to conceive of what is beyond being, you find yourself thinking about what is beyond conception—incomprehensible in a very strong sense of the word. So the Dionysian tradition insists on apophaticism or "negative theology," in which the truest and most reliable things we can say about God are what he is not. He is not one being among others, not one truth among others, not one good thing among others. But then it must also be added that this is precisely because he is Being itself, the eternal Truth, the supreme Good. All of this is appropriate language to use, Aquinas argues, even though we are speaking of a Being, Truth, and Good that is beyond our understanding.[1] So this becomes the rationale for a theology of affirmation as well as negation: although God is above being, it is better to say he is Being itself than to say he doesn't have being; although God is beyond any good we can conceive, it is certainly better to say he is Good than not; although God is beyond all form, we must say he is Beautiful rather than not; and although his life is infinitely rich and manifold, it is better to say he is One than not.

It is from this same metaphysical standpoint that the major theologians of the Christian tradition, most prominently Thomas Aquinas, deny that God can be called "complex." For that would mean he was composed of many parts, which would make him a material being. "Material" is precisely a word for the parts something is made of (think of the "material" you use to make clothing or a building). So if God were complex, he'd have parts, which would make him a material being, composed of some kind of stuff that was more fundamental than he is. And then he would not be the Being beyond being that is the source of all being. So we have another negation: God is not complex.

And here's one more: it cannot literally be said that God is *distant* from us, for that would mean that he had some location in space, which would again make him a material being (only material beings have spatial

---

1. See Aquinas's treatment of "The Names of God" in *Summa Theologica* Part I, question 13, especially article 5 on the concept of analogy.

7 – Jesus and the Church in History

coordinates or extension in space). Similarly, it would be contradictory to say God was literally *outside* space, for this "outside" location would have to be a space outside space, which would simply be another space in which to locate him. So that's another conceptual trap to avoid. The positive side of it is that the metaphor of God being "outside" space refers to his non-spatial mode of being, which implies not that he is located somewhere or other, but that he is omnipresent. Likewise his eternity does not mean he is somehow "outside" time but that he is equally and fully present at all times and places—more fully present, in fact, than any of us creatures could possibly be. For our finite being is never *fully* present (there are so many places and times in which I do not exist), and is divided among different places (my head is located in a different place from my foot) and different times (my past is different from my future). God, by contrast, is always present everywhere as a whole, in the fullness of his indivisible being.

I could go on like this—the metaphysics of God involves a great many important negations, which help monotheist thinkers avoid getting caught in various conceptual traps. There is a beauty in this mode of discourse, for those of us who have the taste for an austere kind of conceptual poetry. And once you get the hang of it, avoiding the traps starts to look like child's play. Take an easy one, the child's question: "If God created the world, then who created God?" Of course the answer is a negation: God is not created. Using the traditional Christian vocabulary, we can say that he is the uniquely *uncreated* being. Or we could put it in terms of "negative theology": the concept of "being created," like many ordinary concepts, does not apply to God.

All this is very well when it comes to avoiding conceptual problems, but it does not provide an adequate basis for religious life. For that we need something dangerously like what you call "the second paradigm." This is a kind of discourse that engages the human imagination, which can picture God as a big man with a beard sitting on a throne up above the heavens. The Abrahamic religions do use such pictures (the throne in heaven symbolizes his power over the whole earth, for example) but also warn against taking them literally. Most importantly, they prohibit worshiping literal pictures or images of God like the idols of the nations. Even icons of Christ represent his human nature, not his divinity, and therefore are venerated but not worshiped. This refusal to take a picture of God literally is one reason why I abruptly dismissed the discourse of "the second paradigm" as paganism.

But there is another and more important reason, which will bring us back to the question of God's strategy. One way we can picture God is as a

Does God Have a Strategy?

chef de guerre, a warrior who leads his people into battle. This picture too is found in the tradition of the Abrahamic religions, though it can no more be taken literally than the picture of a big man on a heavenly throne. And it is found in the Bible alongside a variety of other pictures of God that somehow have to be harmonized with it, if we are to read the sacred text as a coherent whole. In this way every sacred text requires ongoing theological interpretation by the religious community that reveres it. This interpretation, as lived out in the actual practice of the religious community, is the embodiment of its understanding of divine strategy. Those of us who are outside a particular religious community have a right to expect its members to interpret their own sacred text in ways that conform to their claims to uphold a law or rule of action that embraces kindness, mercy, and justice for all. Every religion makes such claims, and we should be concerned, perhaps indignant, when they fail to live up to them. But by the same token, we are in no position to interpret their texts for them, and in particular we have no business attributing to them a crude literalism that their own theological traditions reject.

Reading other people's sacred texts and traditions brings us back to the dynamic of jealous brothers we discussed earlier. When Christians fall into describing the Jewish religion as tribal, bigoted, and violent, then it's time for Jews to start looking for places to hide from oncoming Christian violence. Portraying other people's religion as violent is itself a strategy of violence against them, as we have seen time and again in the history of Christian anti-Semitism. But what goes for ourselves goes for everybody. I think Christians should repudiate attempts to portray Judaism and Islam as inherently violent, even when they come from modern liberals and secularists. For as I argued earlier, modernity has not escaped the dynamic of jealous brothers. The description of religions and their truth claims as inherently violent is itself the strategy of one jealous brother against others (call him "modernity" or "Enlightenment" or "secularism").[2] If I have a right to reject

---

2. For an extended historical argument to this effect, see Cavanaugh, *Myth of Religious Violence*. Cavanaugh does not deny that religious convictions can be used to promote violence, but he traces the construction of a distinctively modern concept of "religion" as a kind of social system, one which is uniquely prone to violence and must therefore be privatized, stripped of power, put in its place and policed by the state. Thus the "myth of religious violence" serves the ideology of the modern state as it consolidates its own monopoly on coercive power. What Cavanaugh misses, I think, is the actual dynamic of religiously justified violence in the West, which is typically carried out by the state on behalf of a "true religion" that it feels duty-bound to protect and promote. The real value of the Enlightenment notion of religious tolerance is that it removed this duty

7 – Jesus and the Church in History

such anti-Jewish discourse in my own tradition, I have a right to reject it as a description of Judaism when I hear it from liberals and secularists.

We all, in fact, have right to reject such discourse, and indeed a duty. We ought not to talk about each other this way. We ought, on the contrary, to expect the best of each other—to demand that every religion live up to its own claims to uphold justice, mercy, and kindness. And in each case, we must start with our own tradition, demanding that those who share our beliefs live up to the best in our tradition and repudiate the strategies of violence and injustice that have crept into it. How this works out in the actual course of history is, I have been suggesting, a fundamental concern of divine strategy, the real strategy of the one true God, whose will is for jealous brothers to become a blessing for each other, a source of life not death.

The various accounts of divine strategy we encounter in the discourse of the "second paradigm" are thus subject to critique from the two other forms of discourse. On the one hand, the "first paradigm" in the tradition of Plato insists that the divine, insofar as it can be conceived at all, has to be conceived as good. Surely the one God must be God of all, and good for all. This is one of the great constraints shaping any religion that either of us could possibly believe. No picture of God as bloodthirsty and cruel can ever be an image of the real God. Nor can either of us take seriously a God that is an enemy of most of the human race. Whatever picture of God we can endorse must be a picture of a *good* God, and like Plato himself, who was deeply critical of Greek mythology, neither of us thinks that the contentious gods who are at home in the second paradigm, whose role is to fight battles for their followers, can be a good God.

On the other hand, the third paradigm also subverts the discourse of the second paradigm by telling a story of the weakness of God, whose chosen ones bless the world by suffering evil rather than doing it—the odd strategy that I keep insisting on, because I think it is the overall shape of the biblical narrative. That is my interpretation—but not mine alone—of the sacred text of my own religious tradition. And I add the insight, insisted on recently by Christian theologians attentive to the consequences of rejecting Christian anti-Semitism, that we can find true life only in the blessing and grace of others, not by defeating them. In particular, there is no blessing for Christians or anyone else in the world that does not originate with the Jews. That is the consequence of reading the Bible as if its center is Jesus Christ, the King of the Jews who hung on a cross.

---

from the state's portfolio of responsibilities.

Does God Have a Strategy?

There are other ways of reading the Bible, of course, and I am particularly interested myself in how rabbinic Judaism brings coherence to the Hebrew Scriptures. But as a Christian theologian I find the most successful way to see unity in the vast and sprawling diversity of the Bible is to add the New Testament to the Old and find the wisdom of the whole in Christ. Without the King of the Jews, the Bible, with its stories and laws, poems and prophecies, looks like an anarchic hodgepodge—it is in fact often treated that way in modern biblical scholarship—where God is sometimes a warrior fighting for his people ("The LORD is a man of war," Exod 15:3), but sometimes brings armies against his own people (such as the passage about the king of the Chaldaeans that you cite from 2 Chronicles 36:15–17) and sometimes brings destruction on both sides of a vicious conflict (as in the story of Abimelech that you cite from Judges 9). The God of the Bible gets deeply involved in the violence of human history in a way that may be hard to make sense of unless we see his strategy revealed in the crucified Messiah. The best way to find a coherent divine strategy in the biblical narrative, in other words, is by looking to the fulfillment of the initial promise of blessing in Abraham (Gen 12:3, which I keep quoting) which culminates in Christ, as Paul suggests when he quotes this blessing and describes it as God "preaching the Gospel beforehand to Abraham" (Gal 3:18). The God who takes sides in the violence of human history on behalf of his people is leading them to the cross of their King, the Son of David who brings about redemption by his death and resurrection, thus leading us to what the rabbis, in a particularly beautiful phrase, call *tikkun olam*, the healing of the universe.

Of course Jews and Christians will be disagreeing about this for some time to come. My concern as a Christian theologian is that this be the kind of lively disagreement that takes place between friends who recognize they have much to learn from each other. Even jealous brothers, I hope, can learn to become such friends. And more deeply: precisely *because* of their disagreements, they should be competing to show each other how the mercy of divine redemption is visible in the strategy carried out by their own tradition.

And Muslims? We shall just have to watch how they interpret their own sacred text, with its own diversity and its own uses of the questionable discourse and non-literal imagery of "the second paradigm." Unlike the Hebrew Bible, which is shared by Christians as well as Jews, the Qur'an is not a sacred text belonging to more than one religion, and therefore we who

7 – Jesus and the Church in History

are not Muslims will have to be mere spectators, as it were, of the Muslims reading their own book. We should expect much of them: we should expect them to interpret the Qur'an as something better than a mere projection of the will to power of ancient Arabic tribes (as if Allah were one of the pagan gods of "the second paradigm"). How they go about this interpretation in the next century or so may turn out to be—or so I hope—one of the great intellectual dramas of human history. In particular, how shall Muslims understand Muslim defeat and suffering (something about which the Qur'an does, after all, have a great deal to say)? If their understanding is anything like that of the Jewish understanding of Israel's exile or the Christian understanding of the cross, then I think we could have another example of what divine strategy looks like in practice.

Jean-François Phelizon—At certain moments in history there comes a great figure who calls fellow human beings to look upon others without despising them, to respect them rather than hate them, to love them instead of fighting them.

Buddha is one of these figures, and I cannot resist the urge to cite some of his profoundly humane precepts: "Never does hatred cease by hatred here below: hatred ceases by love; this is an eternal law." "The world is dark, few only can see here." "Let us live happily then, not hating those who hate us!" "Him I call indeed a Brahman who, though innocent of all offense, ensures reproach, stripes and bonds."[3] In the perspective opened up by Buddhism, love is an experience born from the practice of meditation. It is an experience of openness to the call of *impartiality*, to relate to everyone without exception. A little like the sun which shines in all directions without privileging any one of them, love is not limited to certain beings and its extent is not restricted to certain "preferences." Thus as we make our way in nature, we come to experience an impression of harmony. We feel welcomed to the heart of a world where we belong. We sense then a kind of presence, release, openness, and warmth. We lose all sense of isolation, rupture, or loss. We have the impression of embracing the truth of love clearly and fully.

Jesus is another great historic figure calling us to love with impartiality, as summed up in the formula, "love one another." This message of altruism and charity was totally new for its time, preaching a *law of love* pushed to its logical extreme. Indeed, morality and religion alike are based for Jesus

---

3. Babbitt, *The Dhammapada*, §§5, 174, 197, 399.

upon the law of love. To love God and to love one's neighbor constitute the highest duty and the loftiest virtue, the spring of all other duties and perfections. In this respect, Jesus made a complete break with the religion from which he came as well as the world in which he lived (a world in which the slave was a simple possession stripped of all rights).

It is worth noting that this precept of Jesus is transmitted mainly by the "testimony" of John (which is later, more hagiographical, and less precise than that of Mark, Matthew, or Luke) and above all that there is a certain semantic slide in the apostles' discourse. In the Gospel of John, Jesus actually addresses this message of love to the twelve apostles and to them alone. Later, in the letters that they sent to the believers of the early church, the scope of this precept is enlarged to include all Christians: the *law of love* is presented as a genuine *rule of life.*

Hence, "A new commandment I give to you, that you love one another: just as I have loved you" (John 13:34). "This is my commandment, that you love one another as I have loved you" (John 15:12). "These things I command you, so that you will love one another" (John 15:17). "Owe no one anything, except to love each other" (Rom 13:8). "You yourselves have been taught by God to love one another" (1 Thess 4:9). "Love one another earnestly from a pure heart" (1 Pet 1:22). "For this is the message that you have heard from the beginning, that we should love one another" (1 John 3:11). "Let us love one another, for love is from God, and whoever loves has been born of God and knows God" (1 John 4:7). "If God so loved us, we also ought to love one another" (1 John 4:11). "If we love one another, God abides in us and his love is perfected in us" (1 John 4:12).

Of course, the simple message "love one another," which makes Jesus an innovative figure (and profoundly humane as well), is almost certainly authentic. At least that is the opinion of the majority of the theologians who try to determine what has been added in the Gospels beyond Jesus' own words.

Of course there is a great difference between Buddha and Jesus, since the one calls himself only "a wise man" while the other *hints* that he is "the Son of God." He hints: most of the time, it's the apostles who say it for him. What is beyond doubt, says Ernst Renan, is that "Jesus never dreamt of making himself pass for an incarnation of God. . . . Such an idea was entirely foreign to the Jewish mind: and there is no trace of it in the synoptical gospels, we only find it indicated in portions of the Gospel of John,

7 – Jesus and the Church in History

which cannot be accepted as expressing the thoughts of Jesus."[4] Charles Guignebert adds: Paul and John say Jesus is the Son of God "because that was the only term in human language by which they could intelligibly, if not completely and adequately, express this relation. Since the idea of the direct generation of a man by God could only appear to the Jewish mind as a monstrous absurdity, the expression was, in reality, to the Palestinians, only a manner of speaking, only a metaphor."[5] To be convinced of this, let us reread *every* passage of the Gospels where there is a question of "the Son of God." What do we find?

When Jesus is directly implicated he does not deny that he is the Son of God, but neither does he affirm it: "The tempter [the devil] came and said to him, 'If you are the Son of God, command these stones to become loaves of bread.' But he answered, 'It is written, "Man shall not live by bread alone, but by every word that comes from the mouth of God" (Matt 4:3–4; cf. Luke 4:3–4). In fact, Jesus speaks only three times about his being the Son of God. He affirms it before the Jews who are about to hand him over to Pilate (but before Pilate, he claims to be the King of the Jews, not the Son of God):

> When day came, the assembly of the elders of the people gathered together, both chief priests and scribes. And they led him away to their council, and they said, "If you are the Christ, tell us." But he said to them, "If I tell you, you will not believe, and if I ask you, you will not answer. But from now on the Son of Man shall be seated at the right hand of the power of God." So they all said, "Are you the Son of God, then?" And he said to them, "You say that I am." Then they said, "What further testimony do we need? We have heard it ourselves from his own lips." Then the whole company of them arose and brought him before Pilate. And they began to accuse him, saying, "We found this man misleading our nation and forbidding us to give tribute to Caesar, and saying that he himself is Christ, a king." And Pilate asked him, "Are you the King of the Jews?" And he answered him, "You have said so" (Luke 22:66–23:3).

John's version differs slightly from Luke's: "The Jews answered him, 'We have a law, and according to that law he ought to die because he has made himself the Son of God.' When Pilate heard this statement, he was even

---

4. Renan, *Life of Jesus*, 239.
5. Guignebert, *Jesus*, 124.

Does God Have a Strategy?

more afraid. He entered his headquarters again and said to Jesus, 'Where are you from?' But Jesus gave him no answer" (John 19:7-9).

Jesus says he is the Son of God on two other occasions that are recounted only by John (and then probably subject to caveat). Before the blind man: "Jesus heard that they had cast him [the blind man] out, and having found him he said, 'Do you believe in the Son of God?' [The earliest and most important manuscripts of the Gospel of John have "Son of Man" here rather than "Son of God."] He answered, 'And who is he, sir, that I may believe in him?' Jesus said to him, 'You have seen him, and it is he who is speaking to you'" (John 9:35-37). And again when faced with the Jews who want to stone him: "Do you say of him whom the Father consecrated and sent into the world, 'You are blaspheming,' because I said, 'I am the Son of God?'" (John 10:36).

Everywhere else, it is the apostles, believers, angels . . . or devils who say Jesus is the Son of God. Thus, "The beginning of the Gospel of Jesus Christ, the Son of God . . ." (Mark 1:1). "And the angel answered her, 'The Holy Spirit will come upon you, and the power of the the Most High will overshadow you; therefore the child to be born will be called holy—the Son of God" (Luke 1:35). "And I have seen and have borne witness that this is the Son of God" (John 1:34). "And whenever the unclean spirits saw him, they fell down before him and cried out, 'You are the Son of God.' And he strictly ordered them not to make him known" (Mark 3:11-12). "And the demons also came out of many, crying, 'You are the Son of God!' But he rebuked them and would not allow them to speak, because they knew that he was the Christ" (Luke 4:41). "And those in the boat worshiped him, saying, 'Truly you are the Son of God'" (Matt 14:33). "Nathanael answered him, 'Rabbi, you are the Son of God! You are the King of Israel!" (John 1:49). "And those who passed by derided him, wagging their heads and saying, 'You who would destroy the temple and rebuild it in three days, save yourself! If you are the Son of God, come down from the cross" (Matt 26:39-40). "When the centurion and those who were with him, keeping watch over Jesus, saw the earthquake and what took place, they were filled with awe and said, 'Truly this was the Son of God!'" (Matt 27:54; cf. also Mark 15:39).

Finally, the three last passages of the New Testament where Jesus is presented as the Son of God are the following: "And immediately he [Paul] proclaimed Jesus in the synagogues, saying, 'He is the Son of God'" (Acts 9:20). "Whoever confesses that Jesus is the Son of God, God abides in him,

7 – Jesus and the Church in History

and he in God" (1 John 4:15). "Who is it that overcomes the world except the one who believes that Jesus is the Son of God?" (1 John 5:5).

However that may be, the conjecture—or the fact—that Jesus could be—or was—the Son of God is a challenge for us, for we find ourselves here in the presence of what I have called "the third paradigm": an interpretation—or an expression—of God that is radically new, completely opposed to that of the first two paradigms. The origin of the "third paradigm" is properly sought in the *faith* of the first disciples of Jesus. As Guignebert says,

> Jesus, in announcing the approaching advent of the Kingdom, had been mistaken, and like many another Messianist, he had perished for his dream. But the faith of the disciples did not accept this defeat, and through them he conquered death. They were convinced that he was alive, with God and in glory, and that he was being held in reserve for the great work of establishing the Kingdom on earth. They found a satisfactory explanation for his Passion and Crucifixion. They believed that he was no longer dead, that his wretched (and, according to popular opinion, scandalous) crucifixion had been nothing more than the means by which God had elevated him, in resurrecting him from the dead, from humanity to his magnificent and sovereign role: the Kingdom would be made manifest at any moment, and Jesus would inaugurate it with the grandiose pomp foreseen and predicted by the prophet Daniel.[6]

Why is the third paradigm different in nature from the first two? Because— to repeat—(1) the God of the first paradigm is incomprehensible to our understanding (I have even said that he is "infinitely absent") and (2) the God of the second paradigm should be understood as a projection or revelation of God in the context of a religion; in this sense, he is the "leader" of a monotheist religion, certainly located *above* those who believe in him but little different from them in reality (which is why he can be transformed into a warlord). (3) By contrast, the God of the third paradigm puts himself deliberately *in the midst of* human beings; he becomes part of them inasmuch as he is human, but he is better than they are because he claims to suffer and die for them. (It might be tempting to compare him to a superman, but I think it is preferable to consider him, if I may put it this way, as a "super saint.") Thus the God of the third paradigm "descends" to earth to suffer like "his" creatures in order to "buy them back"; this is the aim of redemption. As you rightly said, "*The God of redemption belongs to what*

---

6. Guignebert, *Christ*, 4.

Does God Have a Strategy?

you call the third paradigm, in contrast to the God of the first paradigm, the infinite and incomprehensible God."

I don't want to get into the issue of the historical existence of Jesus here (attested quite probably by Flavius Josephus, although according to Salomon Reinach, "It is impossible to establish the historical Jesus, which is not to say that he did not exist, but only that we cannot positively affirm anything about him"[7]), nor of the reality of his message and his teaching. Nor do I want to get into the issue of the "genius of Christianity." But to *believe* in this God of the third paradigm, i.e., in the divine existence of Christ (and his resurrection) and then to answer the question of his actual strategy, I think it is necessary to deal with two kinds of ambiguities: first, those that arise from the relation between the God of the first paradigm and Christ; and then, those that have to do with the relations between Christ and the church—the church that Paul has helped succeed by being the first to preach, as we have just seen, that Jesus is truly "the Son of God."

The relation between the God of the first paradigm and Christ cannot be established other than as a postulate, a *mystery*. If God is incomprehensible to our understanding, he is incomprehensible in every respect. This means that if he happened to want to send a message to the human race, this message could not be delivered or comprehended or even understood; this is the direct consequence of his "absence." So nothing allows us to affirm that the precepts of Christ, worthy as they may be, come from the God of the first paradigm. Of course, one can always hope, as you say, that "whatever picture of God we can endorse must be a picture of a *good* God," Likewise, recall that for Plato, God is the cause of all good and he cannot be the cause of any evil.[8] And for Thomas Aquinas, "God is good," "God is Goodness itself," and "There cannot be evil in God."[9] But can we really know this? If we cannot speculate on the nature of God, if no one can claim to know or describe the supreme Being, then how is it possible to say that he is good? The relation between the God of the first paradigm and Christ is still only guesswork, not on account of Christ but precisely on account of his *being* the God of the first paradigm.

The relation between Christ and the church should be looked at critically, at least on the historical level (if not also on the theological level), because the image of Christ has been subject to numerous "apologetic

---

7. As cited by Daniel-Rops, *Jesus and His Times*, 605.
8. Plato, *Republic*, in *Complete Works*, 2:379.
9. Aquinas, *Summa contra Gentiles*, vol. 1, questions 37–39.

7 – Jesus and the Church in History

expurgations" as well as "christological elaborations," in the terms used by Charles Guignebert,[10] who points out that many incidents in the Gospels "seem, to an unbiased critic, to be of extremely dubious historicity, or even entirely incredible, and amongst these we may unhesitatingly include the vision of the Baptism, the Temptation, the Transfiguration and, in the opinion of the writer, the scene on Gethsemane."[11] For Daniel-Rops likewise, "many of the Old Testament references woven into the thread of the discourses of Jesus are probably not in fact actual quotations by Jesus but a sort of concordance instituted by very ancient tradition. In other words, we cannot always be sure whether Jesus directly cited certain passages or whether the narrator of the Gospel, anxious to clarify the teaching, instanced them as a kind of reference. This is also probably true of many comments upon the actual events of Christ's life."[12] From such expansions, such imprecision, such *unease* shared by unbelievers as well as believers, is it not legitimate to conclude that Jesus may be a man divinized by his followers rather than God become man?

To a large extent, Christ has actually been created by the church. The fact is that the Gospels are not in any way historical accounts. They belong to a type of literature in which the factual unreality of the narrative was justified by the deep sincerity of the writers' feelings, and vagueness, or definite inaccuracy of detail were effaced by the truth of the general impression. The attribution of a miracle sanctified by tradition and regarded as evidential, or of a striking moral characteristic, to an entirely different place, date or personage from its original connexion, is a recognized form of procedure in writings intended for edification. Such methods may be rightly regarded as *the first essays in Christian hagiography.*

The church has undeniably been constructed on the basis of the testimony of the apostles—that is, on the basis of the authority of Peter and the militancy of Paul. That is its "genius." Now, the teaching of Christ cannot be yoked—or can only be yoked badly—to any form of compromise with power. By accustoming itself more and more to secular life and politics and honor, *by becoming a power itself,* the church militant has gradually attenuated that teaching (when it hasn't flatly denied it). As one famous defender of Catholicism and "the genius of Christianity" puts it:

---

10. Guignebert, *Jesus*, 145.
11. Ibid., 175.
12. Daniel-Rops, *Jesus and His Times*, 416.

Does God Have a Strategy?

> The *Church* was constituted as a monarchy (elective and representative) and the *Christian community* as a republic. In the one, everything was obedience and distinction of rank; in the other, everything was liberty and equality. Hence the twofold influence of the clergy, who on the one hand joined the aristocracy in their doctrine of power and subordination, and on the other hand satisfied the people with their principles of independence and evangelical leveling. Hence also the contradictory language: before rulers, the priest was the tribune of the Christian republic, reminding them of the Redeemer's preference for the poor and afflicted over the rich and fortunate; yet before the people the same priest was the agent of the monarchy of the Church, preaching submission and commanding them to render unto Caesar what is Caesar's.[13]

As a matter of fact, the result is that the church has ended up obscuring the third paradigm by promoting, then highlighting, a God of the second paradigm who demands absolute obedience from his representatives on earth. (Obedience, along with poverty and chastity, is one of three vows professed by members of Catholic religious orders. Absolute obedience *perinde ac cadaver*, i.e., "to the will of God and the pope" is one of the obligations binding on members of the order of Jesuits.) The paradox of the *temporal* church (inscribed in the history of the past twenty centuries) is that she refers constantly to Christ *in her words*, but *in her actions* she honors a different, strikingly aggressive God, who chooses those on his own side, and who ultimately gives those who believe in him the right to *take advantage* of his name. Is it not a stunning moral subversion when Jesus' original message of love, "love one another," could be transformed by a pope who was unmistakably a warlord into: "Kill them all. God will recognize his own."

It is hard to discern the teaching of the Gospels in the overall action of the church militant. We must recall here some words of Christ, for example those which Matthew reports to us: "Look at the birds of the air; they neither sow nor reap nor gather into barns, and yet your heavenly father feeds them. Are you not of more value than they?" (6:26). "Therefore do not be anxious about tomorrow, for tomorrow will be anxious for itself. Sufficient for the day is its own trouble" (6:34). "Go and learn what this means: 'I desire mercy, and not sacrifice.' For I came not to call the righteous but sinners" (9:13). "If you forgive others their trespasses, your heavenly father will also forgive you" (6:14), etc. Of course, if the history of the church down to our day does not appear truly in line with the teaching of Christ,

---

13. Translated from Chateaubriand, *Essais sur les Révolutions*, 318.

7 – Jesus and the Church in History

this does not mean the "genius of Christianity" has not produced many historic figures worthy of admiration.

You write that the God of the third paradigm "became one of the defeated of this world." It seems to me that here again we must contrast theology and history. If we relinquish the viewpoint of the theologian for a moment and take up that of the historian, the God of the third paradigm looks very isolated: despite the historical success of the church (due to the fact, again, that in its discovery of power it has become fundamentally militant), Jesus remains a great witness of his time, if not a "messenger." Doubtless he is not tied to the God of the first paradigm by sonship (to believe that would be to risk "lowering" God) but he is no more tied to the God of the second paradigm promoted historically by the church, i.e. to a militant projection of God very similar to that stemming from the Bible or the Qur'an. When I read, "*According to Christian theology, the blood of Christ is the price of the ransom paid by God to redeem his creation from the power of evil, which has won an initial victory,*" I do not doubt that this may be true theologically, but as I understand these words ("price," "ransom," "power of evil," "victory") their connotation seems terribly human. In the end, is not Christ in his wisdom closer to the Buddha than to a warlord seeking to overcome "the forces of evil"?

Even with his divine trappings removed, Christ is still a major historical figure. To speak the truth, to share, to love others—these are actually new messages in direct contrast to the 613 laws of the Pentateuch—and to many legal pronouncements scattered throughout the Qur'an. And the "touching simplicity" of these messages is capable of converting the most stubborn souls. It is clear that "love one another" can constitute an *ideal of life* for the whole human race and also a *rule of life* for those who are a bit cut off from the world, a bit utopian, living by preference in a closed community. But why would this ideal be divine in nature? As I mentioned, such messages of peace have been powerfully delivered at certain moments of history; they refer to a type of universal concept that Buddha or Confucius had already discovered in their time, some centuries before the birth of Christ. In this regard, what separates the manner of life of a Buddhist community from that of a Franciscan community, other than the ritual by which they both are bound?

Thus what happens is as if the church, paradoxically, had hidden the third paradigm in order to promote the second. Becoming agonistic and militant, it has considerably enhanced its power. And becoming powerful,

Does God Have a Strategy?

it has gradually fashioned a representation of God derived from the second paradigm; it has certainly given a meaning, a content to this projection of God, but it has changed its nature—without always noticing. This change of paradigm is announced in scarcely veiled terms when the Letter to the Hebrews says: "Without faith it is impossible to please him, for whoever would draw near to God must believe that he exists" (11:6). In other words, every human being *ought* to believe in God. Little by little, believing in God, being baptized, and practicing religion have, after this change of paradigm, turned into *obligations*. And faith has become a way of possessing what one could only hope for, a means of approaching what one could only have glimpsed. In short, *the act of faith has been rationalized by theology, which implies that it is opposed to the lessons of history, which are idealized by the same theology.*

Note that the Qur'an appears to be a bit more subtle: "If thy Lord willed, all who are in the earth would have believed together. Wouldst thou (Muhammad) compel men until they are believers?" (10:100). "It is not for any soul to believe save by the permission of Allah" (10:101). "The likeness of those who choose other patrons than Allah is as the likeness of the spider when she taketh unto herself a house, and lo! the frailest of all houses is the spider's house" (29:41).

The gulf between the message of Christ and the action of the church can be shown by comparing the expression of their "strategies." The strategy of God, you say, is odd: it consists in *"restoring his own creation to the blessing and happiness that he had always intended for it."* You explain: *"The infinite God who controls all events in history has not been defeated in this event of crucifixion, which is the death of his own Son."* And you continue: *"He is not like a general leading troops into battle and trying to defeat an enemy. He is trying to redeem his enemies. He wins the battle by suffering and dying, and then defeating death itself."* I am quite in agreement. The God of the third paradigm is precisely the opposite of a general. But one must remember that the God of the church militant is scarcely different from the God of the Bible or the God of the Qur'an.

This projection of God does not merely aim to protect the armies of those who believe in him; it is the pledge of an all-too-human strategy, as you say elsewhere: *"Having become one of us, using means like us, he can fight with us, strategize with us and also against us. He is subjected to all the uncertainties of mortal life and its battles. And he can lose."* From this

7 – Jesus and the Church in History

viewpoint, an omnipotent God can lose some battles; this is not the least of his problems.

Phillip Cary—We clearly need to talk more about history, including the historical Jesus as well as the history of the church. Both are huge subjects that have generated an immense scholarly literature. I shall try to keep my side of it brief by focusing on our familiar theme of the relation of Christians and Jews.

A God who has a strategy is a God who has somehow entered the history of the world, with all its contingencies, ambiguities, and tragedies. I take that to be a necessary truth. But that God actually has entered human history *in Jesus Christ*, so that the God of the "first paradigm" has become also, *and in this particular way*, the God of the "third paradigm," is not a necessity but a contingent act of God. It results from what Christian theology calls divine election, the choice of God concerning historical particulars such as the people of Israel and the man Jesus Christ. I suppose one could call the identification of God with Christ a kind of postulate, though I prefer the theological term, "article of faith." It is not much like a mathematical postulate, because it concerns contingent historical events. And like the claims of history, the reasons to believe it is true take the form of documents and the testimony of witnesses.

Hence the *church militant* conceives itself first of all as the people whose story is told in the Scriptures, the ancient documents of the covenant of God with his people Israel, but then also as the congregation gathered by the testimony of apostles and martyrs, the witnesses to Jesus Christ. "Church militant," it should be noted, is a term coined by theologians rather than historians, though it does have historical consequences. It means that the church understands the historical spread of Christian faith throughout the world as the work of the Holy Spirit, the third person of the divine Trinity, and therefore as a result of divine strategy.

Because of its belief in divine strategy, the church cannot think of history apart from theology. It inevitably brings the two together in a *theology of history*: an account of how God is present in history not only through the incarnation of Christ but also through the work of the Holy Spirit in the church militant, which is now the body of Christ on earth. Belief in the Holy Spirit as sent by Christ to guide believers to all truth (see John 16:13) means that the church has never been willing to separate "the Jesus of history" from "the Christ of faith." To know who Jesus really is, according to the teaching of the church, means believing the testimony of the New Testament apostles who, like Old Testament prophets, speak by the Holy Spirit.

Historically, in fact, the church began as the community that believed the apostles' witness to the crucifixion, resurrection, and exaltation of Jesus ("the Christ of faith"), long before it proceeded to produce the written Gospels narrating his earthly life and teaching ("the Jesus of history"). What made Christianity a distinct religion—one could say, what made Christianity Christian—is thus not the ethics Jesus taught but the church's worship of Jesus as Lord, which is its primal "postulate" in practice. In this sense the earliest Christians are not to be found in the movement of people following Jesus around Galilee, but in the congregations who learned of "the historical Jesus" as one whom they already worshiped as Lord, sitting at the right hand of God.[14] The narrative identification of Jesus in terms of his earthly life necessarily followed, and was based on what the apostles who knew him had to say about Jesus as the rabbi from Galilee who taught in parables, disputed with scribes and Pharisees about Jewish law, cast out demons, healed the sick, and so on. Thus the "historical Jesus," the Jesus of the past about which scholars have been arguing for so long, has always been essential to Christian faith, but is not its starting point. The living Jesus, who is presently Lord of all, at the center of unceasing worship in heaven and on earth, is where the distinctive faith of Christianity begins.

A theology of history is premised on articles of faith, but it includes contingent historical facts which, however differently interpreted, are matters of common observation. Hence, moving a little further along in the history of the church, we have the observation made by Nietzsche, the atheist, that the Jews conquered Rome.[15] This is a fact of history that is quite unmistakable, he says, if you just go to Rome and notice who it is people bow down to nowadays. It's not Caesar, but four Jews: Jesus and his mother as well as the Apostles Peter and Paul, both of whom were martyred in Rome and thus honored as founders of the Roman church. There can be no doubt that the Jewish "slave revolt in morality" (as Nietzsche calls it) has prevailed. Christianity turns out to be the subterranean success of the Jews.

---

14. Evidence of the worship of Jesus—recognizing him as fully divine—is pervasive in the letters of Paul, which are the earliest Christian writings we have, and it seems to be taken for granted as the background to the Gospels. On how to interpret the evidence of early Christian worship, see Bauckham, *Jesus and the God of Israel*, and Hurtado, *Lord Jesus Christ*.

15. Nietzsche, *Genealogy of Morals*, Essay 1, §16.

7 – Jesus and the Church in History

A Christian theology of history must consider both the *cause* and *effects* of this Jewish-Christian conquest of Rome—this peculiar and momentous result of divine strategy—and of course will interpret them both rather differently than Nietzsche does. As for the cause, however, most theologians nowadays agree with his insistence that in Christianity it was the Jews who conquered Rome. Nietzsche, who despised the socially respectable anti-Semitism of Germans like his sister (later so admired by Hitler), loved rubbing their noses in this kind of thing: Christianity is a Jewish idea. And of course he's right. In particular, Jesus' ethic of love is nothing new. When he taught his disciples to "love your neighbor as yourself," he was quoting one of the 613 commandments in the Torah as he engaged in that most Jewish of all activities, arguments with other Jews about the meaning of Jewish law (see Matt 22:34–40, Mark 12:28–34, and Luke 10:25–29, which quote Lev 19:18 and Deut 6:5).

What decisively separated Christianity from Judaism (though it took several centuries to do this completely) was Paul's teaching that Gentiles could be brought into the covenant with Israel while remaining Gentiles. You didn't have to become a Jew, get circumcised, and obey the whole Mosaic law in order to be a full member of the people of God. Faith alone sufficed: simply believing in Jesus Christ, the Messiah of Israel, the King of the Jews. This also made a change in how believers in Jesus talked about love, because it meant that the early Christian congregations were a very mixed group, consisting of Jews and Gentiles as well as all social classes, including slaves as well as their masters (see 1 Cor 12:13, Gal 3:28, Col 3:11). It was rather bold of the apostles to expect them all to get along, much less to be of one mind and heart (as for example in Rom 15:5, Phil 2:2, and 1 Pet 3:8). This is the social context of exhortations to love one another in the letters of the New Testament. People in the church were required to be kind, forgiving, generous, and patient with other people they would not normally like (see Eph 4:31–32, Col 3:8–11, and the famous "hymn to love" in 1 Cor 13, which comes in the middle of Paul's attempt to resolve a series of vehement disputes in the Corinthian congregation). Thus within its local congregations the church was to practice the reconciliation and blessing of others that is the direction of divine strategy for the whole world.

These congregations were not expected to be so generous, however, with false teachers (see Gal 1:9, 2 Tim 3:1–9, 2 Pet 2:1–22, 2 John 7–11, as well as Jesus' vitriolic attitude toward false teachers in Matt 23:1–26). Such people were to be shunned and, if necessary, expelled from the Christian community—excommunicated, in later theological terms. One of the crucial questions for the theology of history is how to understand what happened to the church militant when this duty of expelling false teachers—"heretics," as they came to be called—was taken up by the state, after Christians began to hold political power. This, I take it, is one of the most important *effects* of the Jewish-Christian conquest of Rome that Nietzsche observed.

Before they conquered Rome, the early Christians had no state apparatus at their disposal to use against heretics. This changed under Constantine, the first Roman emperor to embrace Christianity. Yet blaming Christian violence on "Constantinianism," as is often done, is rather too simple. Constantine himself did not wage war on heretics. He presided over the first worldwide council of the church, at Nicaea in 325, and there he met the great heretic Arius, whom the council condemned. Constantine did not execute Arius but exiled him—a political extension of the church's practice of expelling false teachers from the Christian community. A decade later Constantine turned around and pressured the bishops to readmit Arius to the church, and then exiled Arius' opponent Athanasius, the famous church father. In both cases, an empire whose politics was frequently violent and cruel did not think of executing religious opponents. "Constantinianism" did not mean killing heretics.

Almost 900 years later, something has drastically changed when we encounter a papal legate who is in a position to give orders such as "Kill them all"! What has changed is not simply the church militant but its alliance with Christian rulers, which is now such that the state with its military power is understood to have the responsibility to enforce Christian orthodoxy among a whole populace, by force if necessary. The pope's legate was not speaking to priests but to soldiers, recruited from the northern realm of king Philip II of France to stamp out the heresy of the Albigensians in the south—for the pope and the king agreed that this was the duty of the king and his nobles.[16]

This alliance between church and state is at the core of the development of what I have been calling "Christendom." It is a long and complex development, central to the history of Western politics. Loose talk about

---

16. For a good introduction to the social and political background here see Nicholson, *Crusades*, which includes an account of the Albigensian crusade (chapter 4) as well as an excerpt from the original document reporting the papal legate's chilling words in response to worries about indiscriminately slaughtering orthodox and heretics alike: "Kill them. For the Lord will know who are his" (appendix 6).

7 – Jesus and the Church in History

the church demanding absolute obedience—as if it could ever enforce such a demand—obscures the complex variety of ways that church and state (not to mention other social actors such as businesses, universities, etc.) fought and undermined each other as well as cooperated and conspired with each other in the long history of Christendom. One consistent pattern to keep in mind, at any rate, is that the religious persecution that sometimes resulted from the alliance between church and state is not simply the work of the church militant, for it was carried out by the state as "the secular arm" of Christendom, employing means of violence that have always been the prerogative of the state. It is the state, not the church militant, that has a military. So the church, for all its militancy, would not have the capacity for this kind of murderousness without the state. And the state, for its part, has often encouraged religious persecution for its own very political reasons.

So the church is not the villain of Western history—the state has its own essential role to play—but neither is the church simply innocent. You and I are agreed, I take it, that when the church does get into the position of fostering or demanding religious persecution, it is worshiping a version of the God of the "second paradigm," which is a destructive human fantasy—what I have called "paganism," though perhaps the more accurate theological category is "idolatry." It is the kind of worship the church must repent of. And what I have been suggesting from the beginning of our conversation is that such developments as this are themselves a central concern of divine strategy—and therefore, I would now add, a central concern of the theology of history. To put this theology in biblical terms: God has entered a history marked from its beginning by the brotherhood of Abel and Cain. Such are the recalcitrant others whom the divine strategy of blessing encounters, like the father in Jesus' parable who must go out of his way to invite his own son to celebrate his brother being alive, not dead (Luke 15:32). For as the history of Christian relations with Jews and heretics shows, among the recalcitrant others who wish their brothers were dead are many, many Christians.

One lesson I take from this biblical theology of history is that Christians are in no position to be chauvinistic, as if we (rather than the Jews!) were in possession of a religion of love. Such chauvinism has been promoted by many "historical Jesus" scholars since the nineteenth century, who tried to convince us that Jesus' teaching on love was entirely novel, utterly unlike that of his Jewish environment. The church militant should reject such

DOES GOD HAVE A STRATEGY?

scholarship, for the same reason it should always repudiate anti-Semitism.[17] The Christian claim to be a religion of love better than Judaism is implicitly murderous, as well as contrary to the witness of the apostles, who were Jews, after all. The church of Jesus Christ can be a religion of love only by practicing a different kind of politics—not one in which we are better and more loving than others (a powerfully unloving form of chauvinism) but a penitential politics that begins with the first word of Jesus' announcement of divine strategy: "Repent! For the kingdom of heaven is at hand" (Matt 4:17). The Christian kingdom and its politics must be penitential because it is always our own murderousness—our own participation in the legacy of Cain—that we must keep an eye on if we hope to understand the divine strategy in history.

Jean-François Phelizon—I have been insisting on the fact that Jesus' message of charity ("Love one another") constitutes a break, and I continue to do so. It is true that Moses has the LORD saying, "Love your neighbor as yourself" (Lev 19:18) and in that sense, this precept is not formally new. Still, it is no less true that *all* the teaching of the Gospels turns around this *law of love* while in the Bible, this precept figures only once and functions, so to speak, as a kind of guarantee of a certain social order (the "neighbor" as defined by Leviticus was your brother according to the flesh and according to the Law, he who believed in Jehovah; not the infidel, the renegade, and the heathen).

The *law of love* is "buried" in the midst of the list of 613 disparate *mitzvot* (articles of law) that prescribe, for example: not to marry non-Jews (Deut 7:3), not to lend or borrow at interest (Lev 25:37 and Deut 23:20), not to be a guarantor or intermediary for a loan (Exod 22:24), not to depict the human form even for decorative purposes (Exod 20:20)—or which forthrightly require the destruction of the Canaanite nations, leaving no survivors (Deut 20:16-17). We find in this particular verse of Leviticus an aspect of the filial relationship between the Jewish religion and the Christian religion but also, in the other *mitzvot*, all the discontinuity that separates the two. Haggai,

---

17. This is a point on which the church and academic biblical scholarship are nowadays in agreement. Across the very wide spectrum of scholarly opinion on the historical Jesus, one of the few shared convictions today is that Jesus must be understood in his first-century-Jewish context. Consider for example such diverse scholars as Crossan, *Historical Jesus;* Meier, *Marginal Jew;* and Wright, *Jesus and the Victory of God.* Crossan is highly skeptical of traditional church teaching, Meier is near the center of the spectrum, and Wright is on the more conservative end, but all emphasize the Jewishness of Jesus.

7 – Jesus and the Church in History

Malachi, and Zechariah are indeed the last prophets recognized by the Jews. Christ who, in contrast to Islam, is not recognized by the Jewish religion, opens a new horizon, a new religious era. *He turns a page.*

Jesus assumes responsibility for this radical change. Departing from what is written in the Bible: "You shall pay life for life, eye for eye, tooth for tooth, hand for hand, foot for foot, burn for burn, wound for wound, stripe for stripe" (Exod 21:23–24), he deliberately takes the opposite view and declares quite provocatively: "You have heard that it was said, 'An eye for an eye and a tooth for a tooth.' But I say to you, Do not resist the one who is evil. But if anyone slaps you on the right cheek, turn to him the other also. And if anyone would sue you and take your tunic, let him have your cloak as well. And if anyone forces you to go one mile, go with him two miles. Give to the one who begs from you, and do not refuse the one who would borrow from you" (Matt 5:28–42).

Yet if a new era has dawned on the theological level with the emergence of Christianity, that does not mean the Catholic religion hasn't deviated from the original message. In that sense, the terrifying sentence I cited in connection with the Albigensian crusade is unfortunately not an isolated example. The pope did indeed order a *Te Deum* to be sung in celebration of the massacre of Protestants on St. Bartholomew's Day. The *Requerimiento* of 1513 did indeed obligate the American Indians to convert "under pain of the ordeal of iron and fire." And what to say of the *Malleus Maleficiarum*, the manual of the Inquisition that was originally approved by the Church in 1486 and frequently republished up to 1669 (despite, it is true, being included in the *Index*). Should it be forgotten? Should it be *sublimated*?

As I said, the church has not escaped the natural tendency in all religion of turning toward exclusion and intolerance. There's nothing unusual about this: it's a kind of habitual reflex *whenever a human will to power comes into play.* As in the other monotheist religions, the church has not neglected to fashion its own representation of God. It was in the name of this combative, protective God that the eight wars of religion were waged which ravaged France in the sixteenth century until the Edict of Nantes in 1598. Thus on far too many occasions since Constantine established Catholicism as a state religion, the church has succumbed in your own words to the temptation of *paganism*. It is the church that has accepted the criminalization of opinion and that, historically, has permitted the most extreme forms of intolerance to flourish contrary to the teachings of the Gospels. And it is the church that has over the centuries carried out strategies of conquest:

Does God Have a Strategy?

unmistakably human strategies, but presented as divine and placed under the aegis of God—quite certainly the God of the second paradigm.

In the course of our conversations, you have several times mentioned the name of Nietzsche. I would like to return to him, because the apparent contrast between the humility of Jesus and Nietzsche's promotion of the concept of the superman is quite striking. Let us reread his *Gay Science*, aphorism 125 (where it is the madman who speaks): "Have you not heard of the madman who lit a lantern in the bright morning hours, ran to the marketplace, and cried incessantly: 'I seek God! I seek God!'—As many of those who did not believe in God were standing around just then, he provoked much laughter. Has he got lost? asked one. Did he lose his way like a child? asked another. Or is he hiding? Is he afraid of us? Has he gone on a voyage? emigrated?—Thus they yelled and laughed. The madman jumped into their midst and pierced them with his eyes. 'Whither is God?' he cried; 'I will tell you. *We have killed him*—you and I. All of us are his murderers.'"

The madman continues: "God is dead. God remains dead. And we have killed him. How shall we comfort ourselves, the murderers of all murderers? What was holiest and mightiest of all that the world has yet owned has bled to death under our knives: who will wipe this blood off us? What water is there for us to clean ourselves? What festivals of atonement, what sacred games shall we have to invent? Is not the greatness of this deed too great for us? Must we ourselves not become gods simply to appear worthy of it? There has never been a greater deed; and whoever is born after us— for the sake of this deed he will belong to a higher history than all history hitherto."[18] Reading this indictment, from which there is no appeal, one can hardly fail to ask which paradigm Nietzsche is referring to. Which God does he have in mind when he proclaims that "God is dead": the God of the first paradigm? The second? Or the third?

Quite clearly, "God is dead" cannot be taken in a literal sense to mean "God is physically dead." What Nietzsche actually means by this formula is that God is no longer the fundamental source of morality. Hence the despair of the madman faced with the resulting void: by giving up the Christian faith he has lost the right to Christian morality. For in Nietzsche's view Christianity is a system, a whole in which everything hangs together. Take away a fundamental concept such as faith in God and you have toppled the whole house of cards in one blow: human beings cannot continue to follow the old moral order because it too has disappeared. After the "death

---

18. Nietzsche, *Gay Science*, §125.

7 – Jesus and the Church in History

of God" (an event that has actually taken place already, given that God *is* dead) the task is to counteract nihilism, the general loss of meaning and values in the absence of a divine order. Thus Nietzsche contends that the outcome of the death of God is the rejection of belief in a certain cosmic order and in moral values as such. As the existence of completely "objective" and universal moral laws (i.e., valid for each individual) is no longer credible, he concludes we must go further, beyond the Christian values that no one had ever dared to bypass, suspect, or criticize.

Nietzsche adds that if the majority of people do not see (or simply refuse to admit) the "death of God," that is because of the great anxiety that flows from it. To the extent this "death" is acknowledged, the human race is thrown into despair and nihilism gains ground. Yet it also frees man, because abandoning belief in God opens the way to a creativity that uncovers, then liberates every expression of human potential. Since the Christian God with his commandments and prohibitions has disappeared, man need no longer be raising his eyes constantly to a supernatural world; he can give true value again to the world in which he really lives. The human race finds itself henceforth before a blank canvas: the painting of its own existence is unfinished. Man is no longer "painted," because he is no longer a creature of God. On the contrary, man becomes the painter, the creator, the sculptor of reality. He gains the freedom to become something without having to accept the burden of his past. His future faces him like a great ocean, both exciting and terrifying. As he ends up re-creating himself, a new life opens up for him, leading to new horizons; it is possible for him to become a "superman" (*Übermensch*).

If Nietzsche announced "the death of God" by the mouth of a madman, it is because it is the destiny of such a person not to be believed by the crowd. In this sense, the madman in this aphorism is only a herald, a witness; as such he is not a creator of new values. In the absence of God, the madman feels "the breath of empty space" as it becomes colder with "night continually closing in." The death of God drives him mad; it disorients him from top to bottom. For he feels he is foolishly guilty: "Who will wipe this blood off us?" Unable to make himself understood, he smashes his lantern, lamenting that he has come too soon upon the earth because *the others* have not yet understood that they have killed God: "This tremendous event is still on its way, still wandering; it has not yet reached the ears of men. Lightning and thunder require time; the light of the stars requires time; deeds, though done, still require time to be seen and heard. This deed is

Does God Have a Strategy?

still more distant from them than the most distant stars—*and yet they have done it themselves.*"[19]

In his allusions to the Christian God *with his commandments and prohibitions*, it seems to me that Nietzsche clearly has in mind the God of the second paradigm. And he is not the only one. Independently, Émile Durkheim too speaks of the death of the gods: the former gods are growing old or dying, and others have not been born. He is referring to the moral crisis that pervades Western culture, the crisis rightly foreseen by Nietzsche. He is observing in fact the decline of Christianity as the religion of the West and the weakening of morality, metaphysics, and Christian norms. This development exposes society to an acute sense of *anomie* (or nihilism) in which "the traditional rules have lost their authority." In another register, Michel Foucault takes up the Nietzschean idea of the death of God, but he uses it to evoke the death of man: "Rather than the death of God—or, rather, in the wake of that death and in a profound correlation with it—what Nietzsche's thought heralds is the end of his murderer; it is the explosion of man's face in laughter, in the return of masks; it is the scattering of the profound stream of time by which he felt himself carried along and whose pressure he suspected in the very being of things; it is the identity of the Return of the same with the absolute dispersion of man."[20] In more practical terms, but also more provocatively, the theologians Thomas Altizer and William Hamilton have discussed at length the existence of theology *in the absence* of God.

What conclusion about divine strategy should be drawn from these glimpses of the analyses of Nietzsche and his successors? That the God who loses, whose strategy is uncertain, is the God of the second paradigm. This is the God whose death Nietzsche had the prescience to announce to us through the intermediary of the madman. Should this cause us much anxiety and anguish? Not at all. For the God of the second paradigm makes us doubt man himself. His pagan constitution is but the reflection of human will to power.

But what Nietzsche stigmatizes is not so much the morality of the Gospels as the immorality of the new Pharisees, the hypocrisy of those who over the centuries have subverted and overturned the Gospels for their own benefit. I pointed to the stark contrast between the humility of Jesus and the conception of the superman promoted by Nietzsche. But let's not be so sure.

19. Ibid.
20. Foucault, *Order of Things*, 385.

7 – Jesus and the Church in History

By rejecting human conventions, commandments, and prohibitions, by decisively freeing himself, doesn't the superman come strikingly close to one whose teachings are symbolized by the simple phrase, "Love one another"? Fifty years ago, Pierre Teilhard de Chardin saw in the "superman" nothing more than a simplistic extrapolation of the past that took no account of the phenomenon of increasing communication among human beings. He claimed that already the process of evolution was no longer operating solely at the level of individuals. And, as if anticipating the remarkable expansion of networks of every kind today, he wrote that "nothing in the universe can resist a sufficiently large number of connected and organized minds."[21] To paraphrase Teilhard de Chardin, I would say that *nothing in the universe can resist a sufficiently large number of minds cooperating in the context of the "law of love" that originates from the third paradigm.*

In conclusion, there exists a *weak* God who loses and in fact ends up dead, because religions, just like civilizations, are mortal. This is the God of the second paradigm. At this level, when one God dies, the human race invents another, because it feels the secular need for it. And there exists a *strong* God whose teaching resists the vicissitudes of history but whose precepts can never be respected for very long by any form of social life. This God who emerges from the third paradigm seems to me a complete contrast to the God of the second paradigm.

Phillip Cary—It is always fun to read Nietzsche together! And for you and me I think it will prove particularly profitable. As I mentioned last time, a divine strategy is necessarily a historical strategy, requiring a theology of history to interpret contingent historical events that are often matters of common observation. So it is interesting when a Christian theology of history overlaps with the interpretations of an extraordinary atheist. The overlap that interests us now, I take it, concerns what comes after the period that began with the Jewish conquest of Rome (as Nietzsche puts it), and ended with "the death of God." This is the period of Western history that I have been calling "Christendom." What comes next has been called both post-Christian and postmodern, though I think these two labels have their full force only in the West, and perhaps only in Europe.

Nietzsche tells us what he means by "the death of God": it is that "belief in the Christian god has become unbelievable."[22] Properly qualified, I

---

21. Teilhard de Chardin, quoted on Wikipedia.
22. Nietzsche, *Gay Science*, §343.

Does God Have a Strategy?

think he is largely right. He is not talking about God (he is not silly enough to think God once existed and then died) but about an event in European cultural history—I would add, an event that originated in a fairly narrow and elite social class—which makes it hard to take Christian belief seriously. That is a real historical event. Modernity, in a process *internal* to European Christendom (that's why an important part of the madman's message is "*we* have killed him—you and I"), has become increasingly secularized and inhospitable to Christianity, to the point where Christian belief has come to be regarded in many educated circles as irrational, fanatical, or destructive. In this sense Christianity has been *culturally disestablished* in Europe, in a way analogous to the *legal disestablishment* of the church in many countries that were once officially Catholic.

The legal disestablishment of the church is not such a bad thing for Christianity, as should be clear from our previous discussion. A religion has far less opportunity to become intolerant or murderous when the state is not under any obligation to defend "true religion" and suppress its rivals. As recently as a century and a half ago, as I noted, Pope Pius IX, who ruled a large part of Italy, could threaten legal penalties against people opposing his doctrine of the immaculate conception. Such threats would simply be preposterous nowadays. It makes much more sense, in a world where Christianity is disestablished, for the Roman Catholic church to become a leading advocate of religious freedom around the globe, which in fact is what has happened. The end of Christendom has to that extent been good for the church, bringing it closer to its proper role in divine strategy, which is to be a blessing for others.

This is not to say that Christendom was all bad. Like most other historical phenomena, it has its pluses and minuses. The minuses stem mainly from the temptations of power, which are opposed to the strategy of humility by which God shares human suffering and death rather than power and conquest—the strategy of what you call "third paradigm" and I call "the weakness of God." Yet the cultural power of Christendom has also had many good effects. It has left us with the legacy of a residual "biblical patrimony," as I called it earlier, which includes an emphasis on the priority of love, especially love for the lowly, the poor, and the afflicted. More broadly, it is a legacy that upholds the sacred dignity of all persons and grounds the Western tradition of human rights.

It is a vexed question whether the West can maintain this tradition without continuing to cultivate the biblical patrimony, going back to the

7 – Jesus and the Church in History

Old Testament's insistence on God's care for justice on behalf of the widow and the orphan, the poor and the foreigner—the "quartet of the vulnerable," as the Christian philosopher Nicholas Wolterstorff has recently put it. Nietzsche, for instance, thinks the notion of concern for the poor and weak, which he labels "pity," is a temptation that the strong and powerful should resist, because the sick are a great danger to the healthy—psychologically and morally as well as physiologically and medically.[23] And Nietzsche is particularly good at reminding us that in many ancient societies cruelty and suffering, especially of the lowly, was cause for laughter and good cheer rather than pity and love.[24] So the legacy of love for the most vulnerable among us and concern for their rights may turn out to be, as Wolterstorff fears, "as frail as it is remarkable."[25]

This is one reason why "the death of God" makes some think of "the end of man" (in the passage of Foucault that you mentioned) or "the abolition of man" (in C. S. Lewis's terms) or a "culture of death" resulting from the loss of a sense of the dignity of the human person (in John Paul II's terms). Nietzsche himself speaks in more hopeful terms of infinitely open horizons, of a dangerous and exhilarating "great health," and most famously, of a future that is better than humanity, summed up in the concept of the *Übermensch*, the superman or overman, who seems to be something like a new direction in human evolution, taking us beyond what we now know as the human. But in the story of the madman who announces the death of God, this same prospect of infinite horizons is depicted with a terrifying sense of vertigo, as if the earth itself were no longer firm under our feet but had been unchained from the sun, so that we are all straying through the infinite nothingness of space with no up, no down, no center, and no direction. That is one way to see the results of modern science and secularization. But the *Übermensch*, presumably, is too healthy for such vertigo. For him the loss of God, and of all Christian values as well, means not nihilism but open horizons and the freedom to dance a new kind of dance.

But perhaps Nietzsche is being overly dramatic. The completion of modernity's secularization of itself in the cultural disestablishment of Christianity was a huge and disorienting event for Europe, but it has not affected the rest of the world in quite the same way. The West that explored, colonized, industrialized, and marketed to the globe is the modern, not the

23. Nietzsche, *Genealogy of Morals*, Essay 3, §14.
24. Ibid., Essay 3, §6.
25. Wolterstorff, *Justice*, 393.

Does God Have a Strategy?

postmodern, West: it is a West bearing its residual biblical patrimony as well as its science and technology (also products of Christianity, by Nietzsche's account in *Genealogy of Morals*), all of which have had an enormous effect on the nations of the world. I am thinking of countries that have never been part of Christendom, such as China, where the Christian church is growing at least as rapidly as its surging economy. And I am thinking of other parts of the world, such as Africa, where the church has grown dramatically after European colonization came to an end. And then too there are parts of North and South America where the cultural disestablishment of Christianity has not proceeded as far as "the death of God," and the residual patrimony of Christendom is quite strong. In these places, the near future at least does not look like one of pure secularization.

When I think of these places, I am tempted to make a suggestion about the future of divine strategy, borrowing your contrast between "conceptual" and "operational" strategies. God's conceptual strategy is to bless the human race with life, despite our murderousness. His operational strategy is to do this through one chosen people, the Jews, and their Messiah, Jesus Christ. Over the centuries that strategy has led to the great venture of Western Christendom, whereby the Jews have conquered the whole world, not just Rome, through the Jew Jesus. This conquest brings with it all the historical ambiguities, danger, and violence that come with conquest and power. (No strategy succeeds all the time, much less a strategy of humility and weakness.) Christendom may now be coming to an end in Europe, but it has left its mark throughout the globe because of the expansion of Western power in previous centuries, and that mark includes the biblical patrimony with its insistence on the dignity of human beings and the rights of the poor. Insofar as this insistence thrives in the world even among those who have never been drawn to Christian faith, God's strategy of blessing others through the Jews is succeeding. I hope for more success of the same kind.

Jean-François Phelizon—To answer the question, "Does God have a strategy?" it is necessary to be clear which representation of God is under discussion. We have established that there are three divine paradigms, which is to say three ways of considering God. We have seen that nothing can be said about divine strategy in the context of the first paradigm: God's plan, if there is one, absolutely escapes human analysis. We have likewise shown that, in the context of the second paradigm, the strategies of God bear an astonishing resemblance to human strategies—but the will to

7 – Jesus and the Church in History

power they express ends up *killing* every projection or revelation of God, as Nietzsche shows. Finally, we have considered the God of the third paradigm (who "becomes man") but cautiously, knowing that it is basically Paul who has promoted the divine sonship of Christ, but without ever having known him. Should one draw a different conclusion about divine strategy, depending on whether one is a believer or not? Actually, I don't think so.

First let us adopt the viewpoint of the "believer," who believes the improbable, namely, that a God—no matter how "infinitely absent"—has decided one fine day to become man, to die, and then to be raised from the dead: "if Christ has not been raised, then our preaching is in vain and your faith is in vain" (1 Cor 15:14). The faith of the believer is always a bit like "the faith of the coalman." It is not in the realm of reason. It cannot be proved because it is not based on any irrefutable theological or philosophical argument. "To the Christian," says Daniel-Rops, "the teaching of Jesus is not a philosophical system evolved by the brain of a man of genius, but a revelation by God not merely of *one* truth but of *the* eternal truth, that which men have at all times desired, sought, and sometimes approached, but which had never been formulated in its entirety."[26] In reality, the believer accepts what the church says and is afraid to add any reason why this infinite God has chosen to be present and make *trouble* for humanity.

The believer can be an ordinary man like the coalman, the exemplary antihero of faith who is worthy of admiration. At the other extreme, the believer can be a real hero—an absolute heroine like Joan of Arc—or more simply an "athlete of the faith": an exceptional man or woman, intentionally mystical or visionary, belonging more or less to the category of the martyrs of legend or the holy anchorites. Individuals capable of a hundred feats of asceticism, overcoming the worst suffering, strewing dozens of miracles over the course of their earthly lives, have succeeded in *edifying* the masses of the faithful; by their example they convince ordinary believers that complete and total faith in Christ bears up under every test—and that such faith is effective, helpful, and apt to obtain great benefits.

Of course the believer, whether ordinary or heroic, reacts *against* the conceptual and even operational strategy of Christ, and this makes him cross a line: that of making Christ into a God of the second paradigm. The more excited the believer gets, the more he believes that God directs him personally and the more he is indebted to him for the little victories he wins over himself day after day, week after week. In sum, the believer

---

26. Daniel-Rops, *Jesus and His Times*, 399.

Does God Have a Strategy?

thinks of God (the God of the third paradigm) as a being endowed with will (without will, there is no such thing as strategy) and that this will that personally guides him aims in particular at bringing him together with all good people.

Now let us adopt the viewpoint of the "unbeliever": I mean the person who, not being a Christian, finds it improbable that the God of the first paradigm could have come down to earth, but nonetheless admits that God is necessary to the human race. Hence, for certain philosophers, such as Kant for example, God is not an object of human knowledge but a faith, a moral agent that guarantees the combination of virtue and happiness in the next world, and the immortality of the soul is likewise necessary for man to raise himself by unlimited progress to holiness. For Kant, and for many others after him, it is therefore *morally necessary* to accept the existence of God.

Freud likewise thought God is necessary to man. The human race, he writes, "needs a god as creator of the world, as head of his tribe, and as one who takes care of him. This god takes his place behind the dead fathers of whom tradition still has something to relate. Man in later times—in our time, for instance—behaves similarly. He also remains infantile and needs protection, even when he is fully grown; he feels he cannot relinquish the support of his god."[27] Freud moreover is not far from Nietzsche's intuitions. He claims the idea that we are unhappy because we have killed God the Father comes directly from the mind of Paul:

> "We have been delivered from all guilt since one of us laid down his life to expiate our guilt." In this formulation the murder of God was, of course, not mentioned, but a crime that had to be expiated by a sacrificial death could only have been murder. Further, the connection between the delusion and the historical truth was established by the assurance that the sacrificial victim was the Son of God. The strength which this new faith derived from its source in historical truth enabled it to overcome all obstacles; in the place of the enrapturing feeling of being the chosen ones, there came now release through salvation.[28]

I cannot imagine that the unbeliever (who believes however in the *necessity* of God) could not be a humane and moral being. Thus, since the message of the Gospels is fundamentally moral and humane, the unbeliever ought also find that the teaching of Christ, even if it is not fundamentally divine

27. Freud, *Moses and Monotheism*, 165.
28. Ibid., 174.

7 – Jesus and the Church in History

is "morally necessary," and even if the historical life of Jesus was in certain respects a *failure*, as Guignebert claims:

> The Last Things which Jesus expected did not happen. The Kingdom which he announced did not appear and the prophet died on the cross instead of contemplating the expected Miracle from the hill of Zion. He must then have been mistaken. By all the canons of probability and logic his name and his work should have fallen into oblivion, as happened to many another in Israel at that period who thought himself to be *someone*. What could remain of a movement which foundered in disaster after its brief day, without having succeeded in deeply stirring the people of Palestine? . . . Although it is an unquestioned fact that Jesus' dream of the future which embodied the expectation of the Poor in Israel, ended in failure, it is, nevertheless, true that the rise of the Galilean prophet marks the beginning, however accidental, of the religious movement from which Christianity sprang.[29]

In any case, as Henri Bergson says, "It matters little whether or not Christ be called a man. . . . Those who have gone so far as to deny the existence of Jesus cannot prevent the Sermon on the Mount from being in the Gospels. . . . Bestow what name you like upon their author, there is no denying there was one."[30] For the unbeliever, therefore, everything happens as if Christ had likewise defined *by his influence* a conceptual strategy aiming to bring together, by means of the "blessing of the gentiles," all people of good will.

Thus the believer thinks that the God of the third paradigm directs the human race, while the unbeliever thinks that Jesus proposes a guideline external to them. For the one, God carries out an operational strategy for or against the human race, stemming from a clear strategic concept. For the other, Jesus has indeed established a conceptual strategy but he does not have an operational strategy, since no direction for the human race has been imposed by any divine will.

The Catholic Church has probably always been convinced it is following a fundamentally divine guideline to the extent that it elaborates its own theology, its own certitudes, the foundations of faith and conduct for believers, the faithful. As for operational strategy, things are different. Sometimes the "objectives" of the Church have indeed conformed to the general direction laid out in the Gospels' teachings. But other times, the

---

29. Guignebert, *Jesus*, 537–38.
30. Bergson, *Two Sources*, 228.

Does God Have a Strategy?

Church has adopted "objectives" that are plainly incompatible with them. Let us reread Augustine:

> Two cities were created by two kinds of love: the earthly city was created by self-love reaching the point of contempt for God, the Heavenly City by the love of God carried as far as contempt of self. In fact, the earthly city glories in itself, the Heavenly City glories in the Lord. The former looks for glory from men, the latter finds its highest glory in God, the witness of a good conscience. The earthly lifts up its head in its own glory, the Heavenly City says to its God: "My glory; you lift up my head." [Psalm 3:3] In the former, the lust for domination lords it over its princes as over the nations it subjugates; in the other both those put in authority and those subject to them serve one another in love, the rulers by their counsel, the subjects by obedience. The one city loves its own strength shown in its powerful leaders; the other says to its God, "I will love you, my Lord, my strength." [Psalm 18:1][31]

As I mentioned, it has even made use of the concept of God to carry out strategies that are all too human, and in the process has not hesitated to subvert the message of Christ. This began the moment it became a state religion, a religion that was obligatory if not "totalitarian."

In return, the Church has constantly lent its support to absolute monarchies ruling "by divine right." This can be analyzed as an objective alliance of shared interests, or else as a bipartite power, as in the theory of Gregory the Great in the sixth century. For there was indeed a division of roles: the authority of the pope in matters of religion was absolute, and the power of the king over his subjects was absolute as well. Clearly, as with any bipartite power, conflicts could arise. But the double submission of the faithful to the Church and of subjects to the king went largely unquestioned for centuries. It was reexamined only occasionally, and most fundamentally by the Reformation, which denounced the cooperation of the Church with states ruled by injustice and oppression, but which nonetheless preached the submission of Christians to the prince.

It is a real shame that after the reign of Constantine and in many regions of the globe, Catholicism has too often been established as a state religion. When a religion becomes an official institution, its temporal constitution takes precedence over its spiritual constitution and people never cease to corrupt it. The possession of power inevitably corrupts reason.

---

31. Augustine, *City of God*, 14:28.

7 – Jesus and the Church in History

Unfortunately, *it corrupts hearts just as much*. The result of this institutionalization of the church has been that those who call themselves Catholics, or even Christians, have not hesitated to express their will to power by imposing a doctrine on "unbelievers," violating their consciences, and slaughtering them "for the greater glory of God." In the name of exactly what God did they set about persecuting people rather than lending them a hand? "God," you said at the very beginning of our discussion, has chosen "to be *the kind of creator whose creatures can resist him*." How can it be that the people of the church could have chosen, for their part, to *eliminate* those who resist them? How have they ended up denying Christ with such impunity?

Being perhaps too human and not divine enough, the church has failed in the course of its history. Here again, far be it from me to suppose that Christian doctrine instigates hypocrisy, conflict, or war. If there has been abuse of this doctrine, the abuse has come from men, not God. Moreover, the New Testament has inspired many exceptional people (I cite at random a few names that come to mind: Francis of Assisi, Joan of Arc, Blaise Pascal, Florence Nightingale, Albert Schweitzer). One can therefore hope that the church, when it is fully disentangled from temporal constraints, will inspire many other "heroes," Christian and non-Christian.

Moreover, as you have emphasized, it is probably a good thing for the contemporary church that it has lost many of its institutional ties with the power of the state. As it has in fact abandoned the practice of conquest that was its own for many centuries, it is now possible for it to become a symbol of tolerance, which would absolutely distinguish it from other monotheist religions. The opportunity presented to it is therefore *to liberate itself from its own history by agreeing to admit that religious diversity is an integral part of the divine strategy it is defending*. By becoming the champion of tolerance, by welcoming all the "recalcitrants" without seeking to recruit them, by turning in a resolutely humane direction, by tackling the *discontinuities* that separate it from the other monotheist religions, by furthermore drawing near to the great religions of Asia that have for centuries preached the quest for wisdom and the *golden mean*, this liberated religion would finally, after 2,000 years of existence, make its own the message of the one it has always considered to be "the Son of God."

For the primary consequence of the "death of God" is that *man can no longer manipulate the image of God*. If the paganism induced by the "Gods" of the second paradigm disappears, nothing further prevents the

Does God Have a Strategy?

different religions from respecting each other, talking with each other, understanding each other, and joining one another; this "death" signifies the end of intolerance. Might one hope that the Catholic Church, having less temporal power than ever before, will one day take the initiative to reconcile itself conceptually with other religions, given that "the Church considers all goodness and truth found in these religions as . . . given by him who enlightens all men that they may at length have life"?[32] A sort of encouragement for this is already found in the Qur'an: "Say: O People of the Scripture! [i.e., Jews and Christians—] Come to an agreement between us and you: that we shall worship none but Allah and that we shall ascribe no partner unto Him, and that none of us shall take others for lords beside Allah" (3:57).

In the matter of religion, all people of good will should accept the same truths. They should believe in one God, a supreme Being who is eternal and infinite because, since it impossible for there to be nothing before the creation of the universe, no one can admit that a *nothing* could become something. They should be convinced that a revelation of God, far from being sudden and trite, is often slow, arduous, and gradual. They should understand that charity is the only moral attitude allowing them to rise above themselves. They should be aware that every form of religious extremism or "fundamentalism" is a human creation that was constructed only to bedazzle them, a form of paganism that was conceived only to take advantage of them.

In the end, no revelation enjoys a special privilege. It hardly matters whether the neighbors of Christians are believers or unbelievers, i.e., whether they believe or not in the divine nature of Christ. Wisdom cannot receive any truth that it has not drawn from its own depths or supported by its own experience. And God does not reveal himself in books, however "sacred" they might be. He reveals himself only in the development of our altruism and our intelligence. As Kant says, "God is not an external substance but a moral relation in us." And the Qur'an seems to echo in reply: "it was not vouchsafed to any mortal that Allah should speak to him unless it be by revelation or from behind a veil" (42:51).

Does God in the end belong to the unconscious of the human race?

---

32. *Catechism of the Catholic Church*, §843.

Bibliography

Al-Qurtubi. *Fath-ul-Bari.* 6/30. Translated from http://www.angelfire.com/journal/sunnah/Islam/djihad_obligation.html.
Aquinas, Thomas. *Summa contra Gentiles.* Translated by Anton C. Pegis. Notre Dame, IN: University of Notre Dame Press, 1975.
———. *Summa Theologica.* Translated by Fathers of the English Dominican Province. Westminster, MD: Christian Classics, 1981.
Augustine. *City of God.* Translated by Henry Bettenson. New York: Penguin, 1984.
Babbitt, Irving, trans. *The Dhammapada.* New York: New Directions, 1965.
Bauckham, Richard. *Jesus and the God of Israel.* Grand Rapids: Eerdmans, 2008.
Bergson, Henri. *The Two Sources of Morality and Religion.* Translated by R. Ashley Audra and Cloudesley Bereton. New York: Henry Holt, 1935.
Catechism of the Catholic Church. Washington, DC: United States Catholic Conference, 1994.
Cavanaugh, William T. *The Myth of Religious Violence.* New York: Oxford University Press, 2009.
Chateaubriand, François-René de. *Essais sur les Révolutions et Études Historiques.* Paris: Desrez, 1837.
Crossan, John Dominic. *The Historical Jesus: The Life of a Mediterranean Jewish Peasant.* San Francisco: HarperSanFrancisco, 1991.
Daniel-Rops, Henri. *Jesus and His Times.* Translated by Ruby Millar. New York: Dutton, 1954.
Durkheim, Émile. *The Elementary Forms of Religious Life.* Translated by Karen E. Fields. New York: Free Press, 1995.
Flannery, Austin, ed. *Vatican II: The Conciliar and Post Conciliar Documents.* Northport NY: Costello, 1992.
Foucauld, Charles de. *Écrits spirituels.* Paris: Grigord, 1927.
Foucault, Michel. *The Order of Things.* New York: Random House, 1994.
Freud, Sigmund. *Moses and Monotheism.* Translated by Katherine Jones. New York: Random House, 1967.

Bibliography

Guignebert, Charles. *The Christ*. Translated by Peter Ouzts and Phylis Cooperma. Hyde Park, NY: University Books, 1968.
———. *Jesus*. Translated by S. H. Hooke. New York: Knopf, 1935.
Hurtado, Larry. *Lord Jesus Christ*. Grand Rapids: Eerdmans, 2003.
Ibn Khaldun. *The Muqaddimah: An Introduction to History*. Translated by Franz Rosenthal. New York: Pantheon, 1968.
Ibn Taymiyya. *Majmu Al-Fatawa*. Vol. 28. Translated from http://www.angelfire.com/journal/sunnah/Islam/djihad_obligation.html.
Meier, John. *A Marginal Jew: Rethinking the Historical Jesus*. New York: Doubleday, 1991.
Nicholson, Helen. *The Crusades*. Westport, CT: Greenwood, 2004.
Nietzsche, Friedrich. *The Gay Science*. Translated by Walter Kaufmann. New York: Random House, 1974.
———. *On the Genealogy of Morals and Ecce Homo*. Translated by Walter Kaufmann. New York: Random House, 1989.
Pascal, Blaise. *Pensées*. Translated by A. J. Krailsheimer. New York: Penguin, 1966.
Pickthall, Mohammed Marmaduke. *The Meaning of the Glorious Koran*. New York: New American Library, 1954.
Plato. *Complete Works*. Edited by John M. Cooper. Indianapolis: Hackett, 1997.
Schaff, Philip. *The Creeds of Christendom*. Vol. 2. Grand Rapids: Baker, 1990.
Soulen, Kendall. *The God of Israel and Christian Theology*. Minneapolis: Fortress, 1996.
Renan, Ernest. *The Life of Jesus*. Translated by Charles Edwin Wilbour. New York: Random House, 1927.
Teilhard de Chardin, Pierre. Translated from http://fr.wikipedia.org/wiki/Pierre_Teilhard_de_Chardin.
Voltaire. *Philosophical Dictionary*. Translated by Theodore Besterman. New York: Penguin, 1972.
Wolterstorff, Nicholas. *Justice: Rights and Wrongs*. Princeton, NJ: Princeton University Press, 2008.
Wright, N. T. *Jesus and the Victory of God*. Minneapolis: Fortress Press, 1996.

www.ingramcontent.com/pod-product-compliance
Lightning Source LLC
Chambersburg PA
CBHW030113170426
43198CB00009B/601